D1299151

PERESTROIKA
IN THE
COUNTRYSIDE

PERESTROIKA IN THE COUNTRYSIDE

Agricultural Reform
in the Gorbachev Era

Edited by
William Moskoff

WITHDRAWN

M. E. Sharpe, Inc., Armonk, New York, and London

Tennessee Tech Library
Cookeville, TN

Copyright © 1990 by Association for Comparative Economic Studies

All rights reserved. No part of this book may be reproduced in any
form without written permission from the publisher, M. E. Sharpe, Inc.,
80 Business Park Drive, Armonk, New York 10504.

Available in the United Kingdom and Europe from M. E. Sharpe,
Publishers, 3 Henrietta Street, London WC2E 8LU.

Library of Congress Cataloging-in-Publication Data

Perestroika in the countryside : agricultural reform in the Gorbachev era / William
  Moskoff, editor.
     p.   cm.
  ISBN 0-87332-767-5
   1. Agriculture and state—Soviet Union. 2. Perestroika.. I. Moskoff, William.
HD1993.P47   1990
338.1'847—dc20   90-8603
                                     CIP

Printed in the United States of America

HA   10 9 8 7 6 5 4 3 2 1

For my brother Michael
and my sister Gail

Contents

Introduction

William Moskoff   ix

Gorbachev and Stolypin
Soviet Agrarian Reform in Historical Perspective

David A.J. Macey   3

Devolution in Decision Making and
Organizational Change in Soviet Agriculture

Jim Butterfield   19

Reforming Soviet Agriculture
Problems with Farm Finances and
Equity Considerations

Edward C. Cook   47

Lease Contracting in Soviet Agriculture in 1989

Karen Brooks   63

"Full-Scale, Like Collectivization,
but without Collectivization's Excesses"
The Campaign to Introduce the Family and
Lease Contract in Soviet Agriculture

Don Van Atta   81

Possible Impacts of Agricultural Trade
Liberalization on the USSR

D. Gale Johnson   107

Hungarian Agriculture
Lessons for the Soviet Union

Michael Marrese   116

Index   127

About the Editor   135

WILLIAM MOSKOFF

Introduction

In a recent Soviet political cartoon there is a picture of a glass, steam rising from its edges, obviously filled with a hot drink. Only the piece of paper hanging just as a tea bag would is labeled "ration coupon for tea" and there is another piece of paper at the bottom of the glass labeled, "ration ticket for sugar."[1] In another cartoon, a husband plaintively reports the results of his shopping trip to his confused wife: "Again in the store there is only fillet of sturgeon and black caviar, but no matches or salt."[2] And a starkly empty shelf in an absolutely empty food store bears a sign that says: "Food for thought."[3] These all can be summarized by the joke that circulated about a decade ago in Leningrad. Question: "Is it possible for an elephant to get a hernia?" Answer: "Yes, if it tries to lift Soviet agriculture."[4]

Behind the whimsy of Soviet political humor lies a deadly serious problem—a shortage of food for a nation of 285 million people. Forty-five years after the end of World War II and more than thirty years since Sputnik was launched into space, the food situation for one of the superpowers has deteriorated to the point that in many places rationing has had to be instituted for a number of goods.

The failure of Soviet agriculture to feed its people is a function of several interrelated systemic problems. First, there is the issue of producing a sufficient quantity of food. Second, there is the question of being able to distribute the food that is produced. Finally, there is the issue of producing a balanced diet for the population. The sad and enduring fact is that Soviet agriculture has been unable to do a proper job in each of these areas. Indeed, in mid-March 1989 at a plenary session of the CPSU Central Committee, General Secretary Mikhail Gorbachev delivered a blistering attack on agriculture for failing to feed the nation. That meeting adopted a resolution calling for the end of Soviet food shortages within five to seven years.[5] It is no wonder that Gorbachev criticized agriculture so severely. Agricultural production has been so dismal during his stewardship that per capita consumption actually *fell* for three consecutive years: by 3.2 percent in 1985, 7.7 percent in 1986, and 0.9 percent in 1987.[6]

Quite independent of production difficulties, a second major problem lies within the food distribution system. Detailed data for the first nine months of 1989 show that the amount of substandard and spoiled food as a proportion of all food *delivered* to the state retail trade network was 12 percent of potatoes, 18 percent of cabbages, 15 percent of onions, 30 percent of tomatoes, 23 percent of grapes, and 18 percent of melons.[7] And this does not count all the undelivered food that rots out in the fields or in barns or at other points before it is actually delivered. For example, after the sugar beet harvest in September 1989, the beets were kept out in the open for two months before being delivered to factories for processing.[8] Perhaps 30 percent or more of Soviet food never makes it from the field to the table of the ordinary citizen.

Thirdly, the Soviet diet, although generally adequate in caloric terms, does not provide an appropriate balance across the food groups, being chronically deficient in meat, milk, eggs, vegetables, and fruits.[9]

The root cause of all these problems is the economic system that has dominated Soviet agriculture in almost unchanging form for the sixty years since collectivization was instituted. In sum, that system is marked by a hierarchical command system in which farmers have been told what to produce and how to produce it. Moreover, the prices at which they have sold their output to the state never reflected underlying market conditions. Farmers did not follow market prices to determine how best to use land. Instead, prices were set by bureaucrats who often had no knowledge of what crops should be grown, and the Soviet system of procurements, mostly compulsory in nature, constituted a heavy tax on the peasantry. As a consequence, there was little incentive for farmers to maximize production. Additionally, agriculture has been hampered by an industrial system that has not produced the inputs to produce high levels of agricultural output. Thus, in spite of substantial investments in agriculture in the last two decades, yields remain extremely low by Western standards.

The seven papers in this volume focus on a set of problems and policies related to agricultural production. The papers are drawn from two panels on agriculture at the 1989 meetings of the American Association for the Advancement of Slavic Studies and they appeared (some of them in earlier versions) in the journal *Comparative Economic Studies*. The complexity of the agricultural dilemma is reflected in these works by scholars from the disciplines of economics, history, and political science. Historian David Macey, in the first paper, assesses the likelihood of success for Gorbachev's agricultural reforms in light of similar policies adopted during the tsarist period under the Stolypin reforms some eighty-five years ago. One of the key policies was the development of individual forms of agriculture to replace communal agriculture, a policy which is being pursued today. Political scientist Jim Butterfield demonstrates that there are several areas of potential conflict that impose themselves as obstacles to success in reforming agriculture. The problems arise, in the main, out of agriculture's long-established command system. There are potential barriers at the republic level, where those who replaced the old ministerial system are now operating, and there is the incipient friction between the agricultural establishment and the party whose role in reform is not yet fully spelled out. Ed Cook defines a number of impediments to reform from an economist's perspective. He argues that the planners have made an implicit social contract with the farmers, and equity considerations have made them reluctant to introduce policies that could lead to a more efficient agriculture. As a consequence, issues of land ownership and price reform have not been solved. Cook also raises the question of whether agricultural reforms to date have created incentives that are sufficient to motivate peasants to take up individual agriculture again.

The next two papers, by Karen Brooks and Don Van Atta, mainly assess the relatively new efforts to introduce lease contracting as an alternative to collective agriculture. While there is an obvious overlapping of coverage, there is interest in the way Brooks the economist and Van Atta the political scientist evaluate the weaknesses of this newest campaign in Soviet agriculture from the perspective of their respective disciplines. In the penultimate paper, D. Gale Johnson examines the economic effects on the Soviet Union of trade liberalization in agriculture. He evaluates such effects under two conditions: first, without economic reform, and then under circumstances combining liberalized trade policies and significant reform in agriculture. Johnson speculates that with such changes and in the best of all possible worlds, the Soviet Union would not only be able to feed itself, but it could also once again become a net exporter of agricultural products.

Can the Soviets figure out how to make reform work? This is the question asked by Michael Marrese, who argues that the Hungarian experience has two "lessons" to offer the Soviet Union. The first is that changes in agriculture must be comprehensive, and the second is that success in agriculture could have positive spinoffs for the party by strengthening popular support for the economic system.

There is a great deal at stake in the ultimate fate of agricultural reform, and several worrisome questions have to be considered. For one, there is the fundamental issue of whether the standard of living of the Soviet people will improve. Second, can the agricultural problem be solved without reform taking place in the rest of the economy? That is, can anyone really expect that adequate inputs will get to farms or food to the cities if Soviet industry remains inefficient or if the allocative mechanism is unable to respond to the needs of agriculture? Third, food shortages reinforce the socially corrupting influences of the so-called second economy. As might have been predicted, rationing has generated wholesale theft and corruption. For example, in the Kirov raion, 5,200 sugar ration coupons were given out even though the raion's population is only 4,500. Moscow, although it too has sugar rationing, apparently has more sugar than other cities. There have been "raids" on trucks leaving the city with sugar and other food goods to go to cities with greater shortages. Operation "Kol'tso" (Ring), which began on June 28, 1989, and went on for an unspecified period, in three days alone netted illegal foods exports totaling 250,000 rubles.[10] Finally, there is the question of whether the forces of conservatism will win out over the voices of reform. Are the reforms that must take place so revolutionary that they threaten the foundations of the Soviet system, so that those who direct the system sabotage the reforms?

The cold empirical reality is that in the Soviet Union too many people have suffered for too long with too little. If the gatekeepers of the past are victorious, it could well mean that the nation's fate as an adequate provider of food is doomed.

Notes

1. *Trud*, October 4, 1989, p. 4.
2. *Trud*, June 25, 1989, p. 4.
3. *Trud*, January 1, 1990, p. 4.
4. Arie Zand, *Political Jokes of Leningrad* (Austin, 1982), p. 42.

5. For a detailed analysis of the meeting, see Dawn Mann and Elizabeth Teague, "Gorbachev Calls for a 'Green Revolution,'" *Report on the USSR* 1, no. 13 (1989): 1–6.

6. Central Intelligence Agency, *Handbook of Economic Statistics, 1989*, p. 62.

7. *Sovetskaia torgovlia*, special edition (October 1989): 6.

8. *Ekonomicheskaia gazeta*, no. 38 (September 1989): 8–9.

9. Meredith M. Heinemeier, "The Composition, Quality and Sources of the Soviet Diet," unpublished paper, 1986.

10. *Trud*, August 9, 1989, p. 2.

PERESTROIKA
IN THE
COUNTRYSIDE

DAVID A. J. MACEY

Gorbachev and Stolypin
Soviet Agrarian Reform in Historical Perspective

> Were all of Russia's agriculture under state administration, then judging by [the state peasantry] we would all die of hunger.
>
> —T.A. Valuev (late 1850s)

For a long time there has been a consensus in the West concerning the economic bankruptcy of the Soviet agricultural system. More recently, there has been a growing willingness to recognize this in the USSR as well. Today, meanwhile, a solution to the latest edition of the *agrarnyi vopros* (agrarian question) seems central to the very success of Gorbachev's entire project of reform in the Soviet Union. As a result, ever since he came into office in 1985, western observers have been waiting to see what was going to happen in the realm of agriculture. Now, perhaps, we have the answer.

A Brief Overview

The history of Soviet agricultural policy presents the student of tsarist agricultural policy with a variety of interesting parallels and paradoxes. Following the abolition of serfdom in 1861, Russian peasants continued to cultivate the land as they had for centuries before, based primarily on the three-field strip system of compulsory crop rotation. Moreover, despite having been granted freedom from their former owners, both property and authority remained out of the hands of individual peasants. To be sure, individual households were responsible for the cultivation of their own strips. However, for the vast majority, land was collectively owned by the peasant commune which not only had the power to reallocate those strips periodically but also determined the agricultural calendar and made decisions about the crops

---

The author teaches in the Department of History, Middlebury College.

to be cultivated. And even in the case of that minority of peasants whose strips were the hereditary property of the household, such decisions were also made collectively.

Adopted in part to preserve political stability, this system was considered economically unproductive even at the time. As a result, following the abortive revolution of 1905, the tsarist government addressed the task of raising productivity by introducing the so-called Stolypin reforms which, among other things, sought to replace collective or communal forms of agriculture with individualistic forms by enabling the peasantry to claim title to their scattered strips within the commune, consolidate them into a single, compact plot, and then separate from the commune. This experiment was, however, terminated during World War I and then reversed in the aftermath of 1917 as the peasants flocked back to the commune in the face of economic adversity. Nonetheless, and despite the revolutionary government's collectivist orientation, individual forms began to reappear during the pluralist era of the New Economic Policy (NEP) in the 1920s and even received some support within the Commissariat of Agriculture. This new experiment was, however, brought to a halt in 1929, as collective forms once again became the order of the day, though now they were combined with the theoretically more productive collective forms of cultivation as well.

While Stalin undoubtedly saw collectivization as resolving the *agrarnyi vopros* once and for all, problems nonetheless continued. In the aftermath of World War II, new efforts were begun to address the still unresolved issues of agricultural efficiency and productivity. It was at this time that Soviet agrarian policy began its seemingly endless oscillations between juggling investment priorities and administrative reorganizations in its search for solutions. However, it would seem that finally, after a number of false starts, the year 1989 saw the abandonment of this now traditional Soviet approach and the introduction of a new and innovative approach that seeks to face head-on the eternal dilemmas of costs and incentives as well as the related issue of management.[1]

This is not to deny the many precedents for this new policy. However, with the exception of NEP, most of these innovations were introduced as experiments in limited geographical areas but were never applied on a nationwide scale. The reforms now being proposed, on the other hand, are different in a number of ways and seem more to resemble NEP than the experiments of the 1950s and 1960s. Briefly, the new policy seeks to abolish the command-administrative system of administration, in place since the onset of collectivization, and to substitute new forms of rural organization. The essence of this change is to permit the development, on the one hand, of individual, family, and group leasing of land, and, on the other, of a cooperative system for the organization of procurement, supply, and distribution at higher levels. The goal, it would seem, is to transform the collective farm worker back into a peasant by making him once again the *khoziain* (boss) of the land.

The Stolypin and Gorbachev Reforms Compared

Although it may appear anachronistic for a historian of Russia's first attempt to restructure the forms of land organization and use with the goal of increasing agricultural efficiency and productivity to comment on the current round of reform, circumstances do sometimes arise when past and present are able to throw an especially strong light on each other and enhance one's understanding of both periods. Such may, indeed, be the case with the Stolypin reforms and the current reforms under Gorbachev. Thus, paradoxically, a comparison between the two reforms may actually throw some light on what to expect as we watch the current program unfold. Such a comparison may be even more appropriate since we know not only that Stolypin is currently in high favor in the Soviet Union but that following Gorbachev's assignment to the Politburo, he himself commissioned several dozen task forces to examine various questions, one of which was none other than the Stolypin reforms.

Indeed, the historian has a strong sense of *dejà vu* as he looks at the current attempts at reform because there are so many points of similarity with their earlier progenitor. First, of course, is the notion that finding a solution to the agricultural question holds the key to political survival. In the Soviet Union today, the apparently growing shortages of commodities, above all of various food items, as well as the growing lines that result present a serious challenge to Gorbachev's essentially long-term goal of reforming the economy. Ultimately, such problems threaten to undermine political stability and fuel demands for even more radical reform, including the abolition of the communist party's monopoly on power. Faced with this situation, there are many who seem to think that some form of privatization and marketization would offer a potentially "quick fix" to consumer dissatisfaction by putting more food on the table. Hence, the imperative behind current proposals of reform which are, in part, designed to boost agricultural output and thus help relegitimize party rule.

The situation was a little different under tsarism in that the problem was not so much that of "food" as it was "land." Nonetheless, what was ultimately at stake was very similar: the political loyalty of the vast majority of the population. However, during the final decades of the nineteenth century, there was also a growing concern with the question of productivity that was dictated, on the one hand, by Russia's sense of backwardness vis-à-vis the other European countries and, on the other, by a realization that while population growth seemed to be outstripping the ability of the land to feed the population, industrial growth required a smaller agrarian population to produce a larger quantity of food. By the turn of the twentieth century, however, economic, and even Marxist, perspectives had begun to influence government thinking so much that raising productivity was also seen as an alternative to the peasants' traditional demand for more land. Thus, it was argued that the real problem was not land at all, which was in any case finite in quantity, but income. Meanwhile, as the agrarian problem became transformed into a political problem with the revolution of 1905, a number of leading government bureaucrats began to argue that reforming the structure of land organization and use would simultaneously solve Russia's economic and political problems. At the same time, there was a strong sense among a number of figures that it would do this in relatively short order. Stolypin, himself, spoke in terms of a twenty-year time frame.

Insofar as the reforms' conceptualization is concerned, in both tsarist and Soviet cases the programs involved a major break with tradition, in the one instance with the peasant commune, in the other, with the collective farm. And, just as the Soviet reform was preceded by a variety of attempts to modify the existing system and eliminate its worst features, so, under tsarism, the Stolypin reforms had been preceded by a variety of measures designed to strengthen a "private-property consciousness" among the peasantry by inhibiting fragmentation, periodical repartitions, and a much feared flight from the land.

Third, the Stolypin reforms, like the current reform, were conducted "from above" and were also designed to stimulate individual and local initiative. To this end the tsarist government had to create appropriate incentives. At the time, it was felt that the peasants' desire to own their own land would be incentive enough, particularly as the government had recently become aware of the spontaneous spread of new forms of private property—especially the *khutor* or peasant family farm—eastward from the western and northwestern borderlands. In addition, however, the reform process itself had a number of built-in incentives that not only gave clear preference to those who wanted to separate from the commune but included a variety of grants and loans designed to finance agricultural improvements. Ultimately, like Guizot before him, and like Bukharin and implicitly, it would seem, even Gorbachev after him, Stolypin deliberately called on the peasants to *obogashchaites'* or "get rich."

Fourth, both reforms share a commitment to individualism as an alternative to a supposedly collective tradition. Both talk of wanting to make the peasant the *khoziain* of the land. At the same time, both embrace a plurality of agricultural forms. And just as there is conflict within the Soviet leadership on this issue, so, too, was there considerable conflict over this question within the tsarist government. In theory at least, it was agreed that the ideal agricultural form was the *khutor*. Yet, as the Stolypin reforms subsequently evolved, in part, in response to popular pressure, the government began to tolerate a variety of agricultural and property forms intermediate between the traditional, repartitional peasant commune and the integral peasant farm—though without abandoning their ideal of the *khutor*.

Fifth, at a higher level, just as there seems to be a vision of transforming the kolkhozy into genuine cooperatives that would act as intermediaries between the lessees and their suppliers as well as distribute and market their product, so too were the late nineteenth and early twentieth centuries characterized by the proliferation of cooperative organizations, which many agronomists at the time saw as a necessary complement to small-scale peasant agriculture. The tsarist government, however, somewhat like its Soviet counterpart, was ambivalent about such developments and frequently took direct measures to limit their spread.

Finally, when it came to implementation, the Stolypin reforms were also accompanied by a campaign-style commitment to the new forms that threatened to eliminate older agricultural forms completely—and, specifically, either the peasant commune or private noble land-ownership. Not surprisingly, both issues generated disagreement and conflict at the center.

Just as there are a number of basic similarities between the conception, implementation, and goals of the two sets of reforms, so there are similarities between the problems that could threaten the success of Soviet agricultural reform and those experienced during the implementation of the Stolypin reforms. One set of problems involves both the obstacles posed by existing administrative systems and agricultural structures as well as the seemingly inevitable conflict that exists between mid-level bureaucrats and those at the top and bottom of the hierarchy. These issues were also a problem during the Stolypin reforms. Not only did the Ministries of Finance, Internal Affairs, Agriculture, and Justice come into conflict and/or competition with each other, but conflicts also developed between their agents at the local level and between different levels of the hierarchy within each ministry. At the local level, meanwhile, there were a variety of responses, ranging from an overly zealous implementation of the reforms through bribery, corruption, and the use of correct procedures all the way to complete passivity and a total failure to respond to the rhetoric issuing from Moscow. In the main, these responses were dictated by self-interest. However, some of them were also undoubtedly dictated by opposition to the reforms themselves. Regardless, the lack of administrative control effectively undermined the reforms' chances for success by hindering the development of a relationship of trust between peasants and government. Nonetheless, as time passed, considerable success was achieved in overcoming many of these problems.

In addition to these administrative problems, overt political opposition developed within the nobility, whose most conservative members, in particular, organized as the United Nobility, quickly and vigorously expressed their hostility towards the government's efforts to purchase noble land for resale to the peasantry. In their view, government purchases of land were but an indirect form of expropriation and threatened their predominance in the countryside and even their very extinction—an eventuality that, in fact, Stolypin was not totally opposed to any more than Gorbachev himself may not be opposed to the elimination of the kolkhoz.

Similarly, the implementation of the Stolypin reforms was also characterized by a campaign-style approach which, like the current Soviet reform, included a very real potential for the reforms to spin out of control—what we might call the "dizzy with success" problem. This propensity posed a political threat, for, had it been allowed to run its course, it could well have led to the destruction of one of the regime's most enduring symbols—the commune. At the time, bureaucrats, and later even some critics, expressed public amazement at the scale of the peasants' support for the reforms, referring propagandistically to the process of consolidating strips into compact, integral plots and separating them from the commune as a new "gathering of the Russian lands." Indeed, just as the Soviet reform was conceived out of disillusionment with the kolkhoz system, so the Stolypin reforms were conceived as a deliberate attempt to destroy the "myth of the commune," if not the commune itself. At the same time, the reason it had taken so long for the Stolypin reforms to be adopted was because of the commune's symbolic role as one of the twin pillars of the tsarist regime following the abolition of serfdom in 1861, the other, of course, being the autocracy itself. Thus, any tampering with the commune made people from all parts of the political spectrum uneasy, while those on the right saw political disaster looming ahead. In the end, however, it was the proponents of gradual change who won the day, arguing that change could indeed be successful so long as those changes offered real solutions to real problems.

Then, of course, as Don Van Atta suggests in his paper, below, it is very likely that a major conflict of interest will develop between kolkhoz workers and management, on the one hand, and those who decide to go the route of individual leasing and farming, on the other. A similar conflict of interest existed between those who sought to separate from the commune and those who remained within it. And here, the conflict of interests within the peasantry was so great as to have led some writers to refer to the existence of a civil war within the village. Thus, for example, once an individual peasant or group of peasants decided to leave the commune, villages frequently polarized into two factions, at times provoking major and even violent confrontations with the authorities. At issue, however, were not so much the principles involved as the details. Above all, what was in dispute was how much land the separators were to get, its quality, and where it was located. Inevitably, it seems, when change is introduced into rural societies from outside, it leads to conflict between those who seek to take advantage of the new opportunities and those who want to preserve the traditional ways and hence see themselves threatened by those changes.

A different set of problems concerns the state's lack of resources to assist the transition to private forms of agriculture as well as the absence of a network of support services for "pioneers" of the new system. In addition, there is the problem of start-up costs for these pioneers. In this respect, the Soviet government is in a similar position to its tsarist predecessor in the aftermath of the Revolution of 1905 and in the years building up to World War I, a period that even before 1905 Count Witte had referred to as a "cold war," with all the familiar problems such a situation creates for the state budget. In other respects, however, while the tsarist government also lacked a well-developed system of extension services, an effort was made to rectify this situation within two to three years, with more and more efforts being expended to that end as the years passed. Thus, the tsarist government did make a variety of small loans and even outright grants available for various purposes, including agronomical improvements and the relocation of dwellings to the new compact plots, the cost of which was estimated to be a few hundred rubles, a mere pittance compared to the current costs which seem to be running in the 10,000-ruble range. Nonetheless, the amounts were generally considered to be inadequate (and it does not seem that there were the same ruble reserves that currently exist in the Soviet Union) while eligibility was often limited to those peasants whose economy served as a model for the surrounding area. Availability was further restricted by political disagreements over whether or not to confine aid to those who participated in the reforms.

Going beyond such problems of implementation, Van Atta in his paper raises questions concerning what he identifies as a contradiction between the methods and goals of such "revolutions from above." Such criticisms are especially common among western observers. Yet, in the Russian and Soviet contexts, attempts to stimulate local and individual initiative from above have a long history, beginning at least with Peter the Great. In part, this dependence on central authority is because those changes envisaged by the leadership have generally run counter to the immediately perceived interests of the population. In part, there is an even longer tradition of efforts to combine central direction and local initiative in ways different from the West—and which together constitute the essence of that traditional search for a "third," Russian, or Soviet way. In part too, however, intervention from above seems to be a necessary substitute for the absence of a fully developed "civil society." Today, there is much talk about the final emergence of just such a civil society. Whether that is in fact true and whether it will lead to any changes in these traditional patterns remains to be seen.

A related question involves the relationship between reform methods and the rule of law. Both tsarist and Soviet governments were in the process of curbing the arbitrary exercise of authority and replacing it with greater reliance on individual rights at the same time as they were undertaking agrarian reform. And, just as today, so critics of the Stolypin reforms charged that, in its zeal to implement the reforms as rapidly as possible, the government itself had violated the law both when it adopted the legislation (the law was initially adopted under Article 87, following the proroguing of the Duma over the latter's treatment of the agrarian question) and subsequently during its implementation. At the same time, it was claimed, insufficient steps had been taken to protect the rights of those who wanted to remain in the commune. Finally, there were even some reform procedures that violated those property rights the reforms were designed to consolidate as part of the larger goal of winning peasant trust and support. On the other hand, the obsession with legality could prove counterproductive as the flood of regulations, circulars, and interpretations grew ever larger, threatening to paralyze the reform process entirely.

A key issue affecting each reform's possibilities for success, of course, was the degree to which they conformed to popular needs and interests. In both tsarist and Soviet cases, it seems, the reformers assumed that rural workers and peasants would naturally be persuaded to take advantage of the reforms by the appeal of obtaining land in private property, or its effective equivalent. At the same time, considerable pressure was built into the Stolypin legislation because the government believed that there remained strong popular support for the commune, even though, paradoxically, the reformers justified the reforms on the grounds that the peasants were already imbued with a private-property consciousness. Of course, the different contexts of the two reforms are critical here. Before the revolution, it was not really possible to encourage reform by dangling the carrot of individual gain. In the Soviet Union, however, it may be that the lure of profits and prosperity play a more significant role. Whether that will in fact turn out to be the case remains to be seen. However, it does seem clear that no matter how attractive "individual forms and use" seem to the reformers, they are not always so perceived by those directly affected.

A related concern is the whole problem of equity and the widespread popular opposition that exists to social differentiation within Soviet, and especially Russian, society. Already, we have been made aware that there is considerable hostility towards those Soviet citizens who have benefitted from the new rules on private economic activities and the construction of private homes and dachas. There have even been occasional reports of arson directed at such symbols of prosperity. Similarly, the years between 1906 and 1914 saw a wave of rural arson sweep the Russian countryside, one strand of which was specifically directed against the newly separated peasants. In addition, *khutoriane* were subjected to all kinds of verbal, physical, and even moral pressure by their fellow villagers, most of whom tended to identify such separators as rich or prosperous peasants. The "image of limited good" is clearly not a product of Soviet ideology or propaganda, for it had deep roots in Russian peasant society before the revolution as well.

The apparent absence either of an individualistic tradition or of incentives to encourage its development is also cited as an obstacle to such reform's success. On the face of it, this charge is well taken. On the other hand, it is perhaps less important than is sometimes thought. In the prerevolutionary era, while there was, indeed, a strong communal tradition, peasants cultivated their land individually rather than communally or collectively. Moreover, many observers have commented on the high level of peasant egoism operating at the household level. Thus, it has been argued that the commune was less a reflection of collectivist values, though they did indeed exist, than a mechanism for the resolution of almost endemic conflicts between households over land. In any event, the record is mixed, and both tendencies seemed to have coexisted. Meanwhile, in the Soviet countryside, the absence of individualism is usually seen not only as a consequence of sixty years of collectivization but also because it is felt that all memory of a market society has now died out. On the other hand, however, it does seem that the weaknesses and failures of the centrally planned economy have themselves stimulated individual initiative as managers and others have been compelled to find ways around the system in order to meet the plan. Similarly, the marketing of products from the household plot, not to mention a whole host of off-the-record economic activities and the black market itself, have all served to preserve and even foster economic individualism.

At the same time, it is particularly noteworthy how under tsarism and today, the spread of individualistic forms has been closely associated with the western borderlands. Moreover, in the case of the Stolypin reforms, all of the key individuals involved in their introduction had had considerable exposure to the more individualistic cultures characteristic of those areas or, in one case, to the similarly freer traditions of Siberia. Thus, they seem to have been convinced by their own first-hand experience that greater economic freedom not only did not jeopardize political stability but may actually contribute to it. A somewhat similar case, it seems, might be made on behalf of some of today's Politburo members, though here the key factor seems to have been how far they were from Moscow, usually in a southern or eastern direction.

At a different level, there appears to be a joint concern about the human material involved in reform. As in the Stolypin case, so today, part of the rationale behind reform seems to be a willingness to allow those traditional agricultural units (whether commune or kolkhoz) that are functioning satisfactorily to persist while offering reform as a solution primarily for those units that are in the process of failing. The tsarist government similarly tried to sell its reforms as, in part, an attempt to aid the land-hungry and landless peasants. However, once the revolution had passed, tsarist officials came to acknowledge this apparent contradiction, eventually abandoning most of these special programs that had been designed to aid the poor and enable them to return to the ranks of the self-sufficient peasantry.

When seeking to judge the success of any reform program, whether in tsarist Russia or the Soviet Union, one of the greatest difficulties is being able to penetrate the flurry of bureaucratic paper that such reforms generate and determine whether, in fact, real organizational changes have actually taken place. Even more important, one has to determine whether those changes will actually lead to increases in productivity and output. There are, of course, ample Soviet precedents for such a concern. This was also a problem at the time of the Stolypin reforms, and many critics charged that the changes were simply paper ones. There were, moreover, reports that villages that had apparently consolidated their strips into integral compact plots were nonetheless continuing to conduct their agricultural affairs in the traditional manner. There were also cases of peasants who had left the commune returning once again.

Finally, we come to the charge that the Soviet reform lacks coherence. This charge, too, was leveled at the Stolypin reforms, and for similar reasons. Yet, such a criticism implies perhaps an unwillingness to accept any change as significant unless it involves a radical transformation of the entire system from top to bottom. Meanwhile, as the Stolypin reforms developed, many of the deficiencies in their design and many of the obstacles to their implementation were being successfully addressed. And there is no reason to assume that this could not occur in the Soviet case as well.

Despite the many similarities between the two sets of reforms, there are also at least three major differences. First, of course, there is the difference in historical context, though in fact the differences between tsarist Russia and the Soviet Union, separated as they are by more than 75 years, are probably fewer than they would be over a similar span of time in most other major powers. Second, one must acknowledge that Gorbachev faces a far more acute economic situation than did either Witte or Stolypin. In the tsarist case, in contrast, a market economy had already developed and prices were already being set by supply and demand, thereby making the task of reform that much easier.

Third, unlike the Stolypin case where a reform apparatus was established even before the enabling legislation had been adopted, no special reform apparatus has been created for the Soviet reform. There are several possible reasons for this. On the one hand, it may be that the Soviets will establish one in the future. Or they may consider a separate reform apparatus unnecessary and rely once again on the party itself. Or finally, they may decide not to take an active role in implementing the reforms, leaving it up to kolkhoz members themselves to take the initiative. In Stolypin's time, however, it had been felt that such a strategy would be equivalent to failure since they were convinced the vast majority of the peasantry would refuse to change their ways voluntarily.

Will the Current Reform Succeed?

The ultimate question raised by the Soviet agricultural reform, of course, is what does all of this mean for the future? What is the prospect for success or failure? Let me conclude by making some general observations about the nature of agrarian reform and the process of implementation.

In looking at a given set of reforms, there seem to be two possible strategies: either the government can adopt a radical approach, which would require a clean and immediate break with the old system and would be essentially coercive in nature; or it could adopt a gradualistic approach, which would be slower, more tolerant of older forms and structures, and also more voluntary in nature. At the turn of the century, there were two radical versions of agrarian reform, both of which sought a sharp break with one or the other of the main features of the existing system. The first of these sought the expropriation of all non-peasant land for redistribution to the peasantry on the basis of existing communal principles. The second sought a complete and more forceful and rapid abolition of the commune. And even though the gradualistic version eventually predominated, proponents of both alternatives remained within the government. Meanwhile, although the Gorbachev regime seems to be following the same path of gradualism, undoubtedly supporters of a complete abolition of the kolkhoz and a return to private property principles continue within its ranks as well.

One should not, however, throw out the gradualist solution as lacking coherence and thus doomed to fail. For while the gradualistic approach certainly poses severe social, economic, and political threats to the regime during an extended transition period, it is not at all clear that the radical approach offers any advantage in this respect, since it too entails serious costs—above all from the instant opposition that is created among supporters of the old regime as they are confronted with yet another government *diktat*. Of course, both Russia and the Soviet Union have had experience with this type of reform. More important, Gorbachev, like Stolypin, seems genuinely committed to an evolutionary, gradualistic, pragmatic, and essentially legal approach to reform— an approach that in both cases seems to have been imposed by their overriding need to win the population's trust and support and to build a broad centrist coalition behind the reform program itself. Gradualism, indeed, is an inevitable product of the democratic process with its commitment to compromise. As such, this approach reflects a greater degree of commitment to democratic politics than has been customary in either tsarist or Soviet political traditions.

Ultimately, the question of the reform's potential for success reduces itself to one of time. Will Gorbachev's gradualistic and compromise approach have enough time to achieve fruition? As one looks to the past, previous attempts at reform have either been rather short-lived or they have been accompanied by considerable applications of force. Even in the best circumstances, ten years has been the limit. The Stolypin reforms were brought to an end by World War I, having transferred approximately 10 percent of peasant households to *khutora* while involving close to 50 percent of peasant households in the reform process in one way or another. Similarly, NEP had only an eight-year lease on life until it was ended by collectivization. Collectivization, on the other hand, was essentially completed within a ten-year time span, though under conditions of extreme coercion and in the shadow of another world war. Paradoxically, both the Stolypin reforms and NEP have traditionally been judged failures while collectivization has been judged a success, primarily on political grounds. On the other hand, it is now universally accepted that collectivization was an administrative, political, and economic failure. Only with the perspective of time has it become clear that such judgments failed to uncover the true state of affairs. And only now can one begin to see the degree to which the Stolypin reforms were achieving some degree of success, administratively, politically, and economically, even though they were not given enough time for us to be able to make any final judgment. Placed in a wider comparative framework, however, it is clear that the individualization of peasant agriculture can take in excess of one hundred years.

Thus, as we look to the future, it seems fairly safe to assume that Gorbachev's reforms may well be fortunate enough to avoid being extinguished by war, and to that extent the prognosis seems rather good. On the other hand, the food supply problem clearly has the potential for destabilizing the political situation and thus leading either to the adoption of a more radical approach, as happened in 1917 and 1929, or perhaps to a return to the *status quo ante*. Regardless, it does seem that the strategy of imposing a gradualist reform from above by a strong political regime represents the best possible combination of political and economic factors and holds the greatest potential for long-term economic and political success.

Part of the answer, however, may lie, as it has so often before, with what happens at the local level. And here, it is important to realize that no matter what approach is adopted, it is going to create a certain amount of conflict and chaos. Certainly this was true of the Stolypin reforms. However, it is wrong to look at these consequences and argue that the reforms are a failure as is so frequently done for the Stolypin reforms. Given that chaos and conflict must be counted among the inevitable costs of reform, it may well be that a strong and stable, even authoritarian, regime is essential in order to survive these inevitable conflicts of interest. Part of the solution, however, will depend on whether these conflicts can be handled by the judicial system, as they were in part during the Stolypin years, or whether the government itself ends up being held responsible for the disruptions, thereby reviving that ominous polarization between ''us'' and ''them.'' Ultimately, it seems, the outcome will depend in part on the degree to which Gorbachev's attempt to introduce reform from above is successful in fostering the emergence of a genuine civil society, along with its concomitant, an effective legal system. And here, one must point out one final difference in the contexts of the two reforms, namely, that the agricultural population has shrunk from approximately 75 percent of the total population before the Revolution to somewhat less than one-third today. As a result, the political impact of any rural disruption is likely to be much weaker than it was in the past. Thus, it seems that while a comparison of the Stolypin reforms validates the concerns raised in the essays that follow by Butterfield, Van Atta, and Cook, it also seems that there is less cause for concern than they would suggest and even that the policy that has been adopted by the Soviet government, with appropriate modifications in the future, may well provide the basis for a successful transformation.

In conclusion, it should be mentioned that there is something faintly anachronistic about this whole discussion and about the Soviet reform itself. After all, the family farm is already on its way out as the basic agricultural producer in the advanced capitalist world. Moreover, the tsarist experience suggests that individualistic reforms may not be the panacea that they are sometimes thought to be. Certainly Russia's pre-revolutionary peasants did not respond with quite the alacrity that Stolypin had hoped for, though there was a significant response, nonetheless. At the same time, it appears that the economic results of the reforms were even slower in coming. Thus, it is not clear what benefits the Soviet Union hopes to reap by turning back the clock of history, unless, perhaps, this step is seen as a necessary part of the ongoing effort to come to political and moral terms with Stalinism in all its aspects. In the last analysis, however, it seems that success should not be measured simply in terms of achieving or failing to achieve some predetermined goal. Rather, it is the process itself that is important.

Note

1. This paper is a revision and elaboration of comments originally delivered at the panel on "Agricultural Reform in the Soviet Union" at the 21st National Convention of the American Association for the Advancement of Slavic Studies at Chicago, November 3, 1989. The synopsis of Soviet agrarian policy and its problems developed here is drawn largely from the papers presented at the panel by Jim Butterfield, Don Van Atta, and Edward Cook, which follow in this collection.

JIM BUTTERFIELD

Devolution in Decision Making and Organizational Change in Soviet Agriculture

By introducing perestroika, the Soviet reform package, General Secretary and President Gorbachev has not only torn asunder many of the givens under which Soviet citizens have complacently lived for over a generation, but he has given Western observers of Soviet politics a chance to examine political change in a context once characterized by a virtual absence of change.[1] He has also given us a challenge to explain various patterns of regime initiative that are without precedent, and to analyze the multiple forces that are dictating the course of reform. In this, we must explain not only the whys and hows of radical policy departures from past experience, but also the dynamics of various facets of reform once introduced as they percolate throughout the system.

In analyzing the forces opposing reform, analysts quite naturally focus in part on the elements of the central elite who are either anti-reform or who support a much more cautious reform process than the one led by Gorbachev. This is useful in explaining the seeming policy reversals and compromises that occur from time to time.[2] But what of the course of various reforms once introduced? Why is it difficult actually to implement a reform once it has successfully passed through the obstacle course of formulation and adoption? This is an understudied area. Problems in policy implementation are usually explained with reference to various "inertial forces," usually defined as the "entrenched bureaucracy," "recalcitrant local officials," or "obstructive party *apparatchiki*." But what precisely are the dynamics of policy implementation? What role do these forces (the bureaucracy, local officials and the *apparatchiki*) actually play in the process? What are

---

The author teaches in the Department of Political Science, Western Michigan University.

the sources of conservatism in Soviet reform beyond the arena of power politics at the center?

One attempt at reform that has already run an extensive course is in the realm of agricultural management. From it there are lessons to be learned regarding the implementation process. Various stages of the reform, which started with the formation of a local management organ known by its Russian acronym RAPO, and which later included several "next generation" organizations that both supplemented and replaced the RAPO, serve to indicate that organizational conservatism and its attendant features of risk-avoidance, deference to higher-standing authorities, and institutionalized priorities in management decision making are significant obstacles to the introduction of innovative reforms.

This article has two goals: to demonstrate the difficulties of organizational reform at the local level, and to examine how the Soviets are dealing with the problem. It is a significant problem indeed, because it inherently hampers the food production process. Soviets and Westerners alike have argued that the leadership must do something about the food problem in the short term if perestroika is going to succeed. Thus, the regime has taken a step away from reliance on organizational reforms as a solution to food production problems and has begun to emphasize altering the incentive structure of the farmers themselves.

This article will address the nature of organizational conservatism by examining local agricultural reforms in the period 1982–89. Ultimately, it will argue that the results desired in the perestroika of agriculture, which the leadership has attempted to achieve by tampering with the management structure, can be attained only slowly because of organizational conservatism. Due to pressure on the regime to show some benefits of the overall perestroika (specifically, in this case, more quantity and variety of food products), it has de-emphasized centralized economic management in favor of leasing arrangements and cooperative forms of management, both of which in large part ignore centralized decision-making processes and rely on incentives to farmers, food industry workers, and managers.

The paper treats, in turn, the various organizational formats at the local level that the center has tried throughout the eighties. It will then briefly address the elements of current reform policy which rely on decentralized management and leasing arrangements,[3] thereby demonstrating the gradual transition in agricultural management that has occurred during the eighties. Finally, it will offer an analysis of why organizational reform at the local level has been so difficult, and will offer insights into the difficulties of introducing economic reforms into a highly static environment.

Organizational Reforms at the Local Level

Emphasis on reforming the management structure started with the introduction of the Food Program at the May Plenum in 1982. A raion-level[4] management organization (the RAPO) was introduced, and in November 1985 was strengthened in a major reform which included the formation of *Gosagroprom*, the State Committee of the Agro-industrial Complex. As the center became disenchanted with the RAPO in 1987 and early 1988, it began to focus on several "next generation" organizations, the agricultural combine *(agrokombinat)*, the *agrofirm*, and the agro-association based on the *Novomoskovskoe* model association in Tula oblast.[5] Each serves as an umbrella management organization that supervises either an entire raion's food economy or, in the case of the agrofirm, a number of enterprises within the raion that are logically linked in production stages. Each will be treated in turn.

The RAPO

The RAPO (from the Russian acronym for raion agro-industrial association)[6] was formed to deal with a chronic problem in agricultural management. For two decades the ministries associated with agriculture had multiplied to the point where the farms and agriculturally related enterprises in any given raion were subordinated to up to eight different ministries (each farm or ministry was subordinate to only one of the eight). The result of this branch system, as it is called in Soviet parlance, was excellent vertical communication between farm or enterprise and its corresponding ministry, but a nearly complete absence of horizontal communication between farms, service enterprises, processing plants and procurement stations. In addition, several linkage points in the vertical production process (inputs–production–processing–distribution) were very undeveloped; in particular, storage, transportation, and processing difficulties caused significant losses of produced goods.[7] The RAPO was to be a local-level centralized management body that would cut across ministerial cleavages to provide for integrated decision making and horizontal communication among the farms and enterprises of the raion food economy. But the ministries continued to function and the RAPO found itself in competition with them over authority. In November 1985 a reform abolished six of the ministries and created *Gosagroprom*, which had the effect of strengthening the RAPO's direct authority over farms and enterprises.[8]

The RAPO program was an attempt to rationalize the management structure by removing organizational obstacles which had stood in the way of natural vertical linkages in the food production process. For it to succeed, the locus of decision making had to be changed from points much higher in the management hierarchy down to the RAPO. Such a devolution of authority required three concurrent conditions. The first was the willingness of ministry and oblast agricultural management officials to concede RAPO officials their legal authority. Secondly, raion party officials had to refrain from intervening in agricultural management, a situation that was all too common. Party officials habitually intervened to fill the vacuum in coordination left by the splintered ministerial system.[9] The third was the willingness of RAPO officials to use the authority granted them. Evidence strongly indicates that only rarely did all three conditions occur in any one case.

The RAPO was given broad powers in matters involving coordination and integration, planning, investment, and use of technology. But the powers formally accorded to the RAPO had once been the responsibility of other organs, and those organs, especially oblast- and republic-level organs within the agricultural ministerial hierarchy, were loathe to give them up. The press was replete with numerous criticisms of oblast and republic agro-industrial committees and their constant attempt to continue micromanagement of the raion food economy from their distant locations.[10] The workload of RAPO officials was dominated by the need to deal with hundreds and sometimes thousands of directives, orders, and requests for information that came to them from higher-standing organs.[11]

Further complicating the ability of RAPO officials to deal with their jurisdictions authoritatively were local party organs, particularly the raion party committee (the *raikom*). Party officials from the *raikom* were as unwilling as ministry officials to refrain from intervening in day-to-day matters of the raion food economy. They frequently dictated planting and harvesting schedules, financing arrangements, investment targets, planning quotas, and wage policies.[12]

Concurrent with the unwillingness of party and ministry organs to concede RAPO officials their due authority was a tendency among the latter to avoid responsibility. RAPO officials tended to immerse themselves in paperwork, slavishly dealing with directives from above and, in turn, sending dozens and even hundreds of similar directives to their constituent farms and enterprises.[13] Centralized funds were supposed to be collected in a pro-rated fashion from each constituent enterprise according to profitability, and were to be distributed according to development needs across the raion (including investment in financially unhealthy and underdeveloped farms). There is little evidence that the RAPO utilized its centralized funds in any redistributive fashion (the manner in which they were intended to be used) to invest in storage, transportation, or processing on any significant scale.[14] In addition, in a series of interviews in 1986 and 1987 with farm, RAPO, and ministry officials and researchers, the author failed to find more than a few isolated examples of utilization of funds in any more than a pro forma fashion.

By mid-1987 it was becoming apparent that the RAPO was failing to become an authoritative decision-making organ, and the center began to cast around for organizational alternatives. At the same time, it tried one more reform of the RAPO to attempt to induce it to become both more responsible in dealing with coordinative problems of the local food economy and at the same time more responsive to its constituent members, the farms and agriculturally related enterprises within each raion. In keeping with the democratization movement first discussed in January of that year, each RAPO was required to select a chairman of the RAPO's governing council from within its membership, which in turn would supervise the director of the RAPO's apparat. This built on a brief experiment with such an arrangement in a few RAPOs in Latvia.[15] A Central Committee resolution published on September 25 called for the widespread introduction of a democratically elected chairman that would oversee the work of the apparat and its director.[16]

This trend was underscored in an editorial in *Sel'skaia zhizn'*, the agricultural daily, in November and in a Central Committee conference a few days later.[17] Central Committee Secretary Victor Nikonov claimed at that time the new ''democratic'' council was functioning in some raions in Latvia, Estonia, Stavropol krai, and in Volgograd, Rostov and "several other" oblasts, and preliminary evaluation offered very high hopes for this new form.

Yet, after the end of 1987, there was a marked absence of any further commentary in the press. One can only surmise the reason for this. Either many raions simply did not implement the new democratic form, or they did and it had no effect. Even before Nikonov was pronouncing the advantages of the new, more "democratic" RAPO, the center was already lauding an alternative raion-level organization, the *agrokombinat,* and was closely watching yet another, the agrofirm.

Complete dissatisfaction with the RAPO's inability to become an authoritative decision-making organ was indicated by Gorbachev himself at both the June Conference and the July Central Committee Plenum of 1988. In sounding the death knell of the RAPO, he claimed that it was not functioning as intended; he argued that it was "redundant," and that serious thought should be given to different approaches.[18] The final pronouncement on the RAPO's fate awaited the long-delayed Central Committee Plenum finally held in March 1989, when the RAPO program was formally disbanded.[19]

The Agrokombinat

The first "next generation" agricultural management organization to appear on the scene was the agricultural combine, or *agrokombinat.* It got its start in Dagestan in the early eighties with a kombinat entitled *Nagornyi Dagestan.* While the Dagestan kombinat never received much publicity, another agrokombinat in neighboring Krasnodar krai[20] served as the model from which future agrokombinats were fashioned. The *Kuban'* agrokombinat was formed in 1983 in Timeshevskii raion, and encompassed every agricultural and agriculturally related enterprise in the raion.[21]

One of the innovative features of the agrokombinat is its internal banking system (referred to as a financial-accounting center), which gives it much more control over disbursement of internal financial resources such as loan monies, profits, and centralized funds. The other unique feature, retail stores, can actually extend the agrokombinat beyond its nominal territorial base. The *Kuban'* agrokombinat has stores in Krasnodar and Sochi (respectively, the major urban center of the krai and one of the most famous resort areas in the

Soviet Union) and two other cities in the krai. The Ramenskii agrokombinat in Moscow oblast has stores operating in Moscow. This, according to its proponents, raises the agrokombinat to the highest stage in agro-industrial integration: one management body that controls the entire process of agricultural inputs, production, processing, storage, transportation, and sale.

The agrokombinat gained increasing attention in the autumn of 1986 with, first, a visit by Gorbachev to the northern Caucausus which included an inspection of the *Kuban'*[22] and a subsequent meeting of the Politburo approving the model and calling for the formation of 14 additional agrokombinats in the Russian, Ukrainian, and Belorussian republics. About the same time, articles appeared in *Ekonomicheskaia gazeta* detailing the experiment in Krasnodar and the newer agrokombinat Ramenskii, which had been operating long enough to supply an additional model,[23] and which was the subject of a later visit by Gorbachev.[24] A number of agrokombinats were quickly formed, surpassing both the original number called for in the October 1986 Politburo meeting and the locations in which they were to be formed.[25] Increasing attention was being devoted to the agrokombinat at the same time that the center was gradually abandoning its hopes for the RAPO.

The Agrofirm

Another organizational innovation is the agrofirm, which had its inception in Latvia with the assistance of the same specialist who was the intellectual force behind one of the experimental RAPOs. The agrofirm is much like the agrokombinat except that it is more limited in scale, encompassing only a few enterprises all related to one or two specialties. The model agrofirm is Adazhi, located about one half hour outside of Riga. Formed in mid-1986 on the basis of a longstanding model kolkhoz, it expanded its primary activities of production and sale of high-quality seed potatoes, milk, and fur to include processing of meat products (although as yet it has no full-scale meat packing plant—only a couple of small shops for making kielbasa) and potatoes. Indeed, the latter has grown to include the production of potato sticks which are immensely popular in Riga and other cities and mark one of the first ventures into "junk food" by the Soviets. Other processing ventures are planned.[26]

While Adazhi was steadily developing its own processing base, three other agrofirms in Latvia were formed by combining several farms, processing plants, and stores.[27] They specialized in a variety of agricultural and food products, including fruit and vegetables, meat, dairy, and flax. By late 1988 at least nine agrofirms had been formed across the country.[28] This was in part due to Gorbachev's highly publicized visit to Adazhi earlier in February 1987.[29]

Like the *agrokombinat,* the agrofirm is also engaged in both processing and retail ventures. In Mogilev oblast the agrofirm "Rassvet" has processing capacity for dairy, meat, and fruit products, as well as stores in three of the largest cities in the oblast.[30] In Ekabpils, Latvia, a new store was recently built to handle one agrofirm's processed goods, which include dairy products, kielbasa, fresh vegetables, canned goods, juices, and candy.[31] Thus, both the agrokombinat and the agrofirm have as primary goals integration of service, production and processing (a largely unfulfilled goal of the RAPO), and marketing of consumer-ready food products.

The Agro-association

In Novomoskovskii raion in Tula oblast, a new-style agro-industrial association started operations in April 1987. The Novomoskovskoe agro-association is distinct from the RAPO, and both the leadership and the media were careful to maintain that distinction so as to avoid conferring the RAPO's increasingly poorer reputation on the new form of association.

On one occasion the Novomoskovskoe agro-industrial association was referred to as "a unique type of socialist joint-stock company."[32] The association was managed by an apparat considerably smaller than the combined RAPO and farm/enterprise apparats, and "the command-bureaucratic style of the pre-existing RAPO . . . disappeared."[33] Within the association there were several councils and cooperative bodies which coordinated similar activities among the farms and enterprises. For example, the chief engineers of each farm and enterprise came together in a group to form the governing body of a cooperative maintenance organization, called the productive-technical cooperative.[34] The cooperative had its own permanent staff and worked on a contractual basis with farms and enterprises. The profits from this and other cooperatives (there were four—besides the maintenance co-op there were crop production, dairy/meat, and construction coopera-tives)[35] were distributed among the members of the association, with a small sum going to the association (limited to 5 percent) for adminis-trative costs.[36]

Other Raion-level Management Organizations

While the RAPO has been formally disbanded due to its debilitating reputation as an ineffective management organ that represented cen-tralization at a time when decentralization is becoming the vogue, the other three organizations described in the preceding paragraphs (the agrokombinat, the agrofirm, and the agro-association) are currently being touted as the wave of the future in raion management. Agricul-tural secretary Nikonov[37] claimed in early 1989 that over 330 agro-in-dustrial combines and agrofirms were operating in the country.[38] That figure represents a significant increase since late summer 1988, when the number was probably no more than fifty. But they are not being treated as exclusive options; that is, they are not mandated for all raions throughout the country as was the RAPO. Indeed, several areas are experimenting with other forms of raion-level management.

One such experiment is referred to as a "union of cooperatives." The model is located in Sverdlovsk oblast and is conducted at the raion level.[39] The farms have been turned into "associations of coopera-tives," in which work is organized into small cooperatives that have responsibility for one or more facets of agricultural production. The management structure of the farms and of the raion unions are all formed on a cooperative basis. This is much like the Novomoskovskii agro-association model, except in the latter the cooperative manage-ment organs do not extend to the farm management structure. At the oblast level, a cooperative association was formed with subdivisions that coincide with the structural subdivisions at the raion and farm level. Some of the subdivisions are traditional: agronomy, animal hus-bandry, machinery repair, agrochemical service, construction, land rec-lamation, finance, legal consulting, and veterinary. Others are less traditional: one subdivision provides scientific and technical assis-tance, and another handles the commercial aspects of the unions. The retailing ventures of the union liken it to both the agro-industrial com-bine and the agrofirm.

As can be seen, as each new organizational format is introduced, the emphasis is to move away from centralized management at the raion level (as represented by the RAPO) toward more loosely "confederated" management organizations which are cooperative in character and therefore more decentralized. What does this mean for farm management, and how do the new management priorities fit in with the leasing program?

Farm Management and Leases

The primary enterprises in agriculture, the kolkhoz and sovkhoz, continue to exist despite some discussion about their continuing utility.[40] But even though they have been maintained, there are some significant departures of late. First of all, the differentiation between the two may be more substantive than has actually been for years. This is due largely to the reassertion of cooperative forms of ownership in the economy, which was the primary theme of the kolkhoz congress of March 1988. Kolkhozes, which are supposed to be managed according to the cooperative principle by a chairman and a democratically elected council, may in fact become the cooperatives they were supposed to be under collectivization. But there are other differences as well, and they relate primarily to two different factors: the leasing program and the continuing problem with financially unhealthy farms.

The leasing program is the most significant innovation in agricultural policy in decades. Families and small groups may lease land from the state and operate it in many ways like private farmers in the West. It has not been clear for some time exactly what the role of the farm would be if leases were implemented on a grand scale. Now, as of the March 1989 Plenum, it is clear that the farm is the primary leasing agent, and even in those cases in which the farm would lease out all of its land, it would still function to administer the leases, supervise the distribution of equipment, provide agronomical and veterinary services, and manage intrafarm storage and transportation. The term "cooperative of lessees" has been used to describe such a situation. It is not likely, however, that many farms will be given over wholly to leases, but Gorbachev left the door open for that possibility in one of his speeches at the plenum.[41] Therefore the traditional tasks of farm management will continue to exist alongside the new cooperative lease management functions.

A second innovation in farm management deals with the longstanding problems of farms which perennially operate at a loss. One attempt to deal with this problem was the increase in procurement prices in 1982; they are to be raised again as a result of the 1989 reform. Another attempt involved several redistributive funds of the RAPO, which were to be collected from wealthier farms and processing enterprises and reallocated into the infrastructure of lagging farms. The latter attempt did not work, as RAPO officials were unwilling or unable to redistribute the wealth of the raion in the face of fierce resistance on the part of the wealthier farms.[42] A March 1986 decree that allowed farms to sell portions of their produce at the farmers markets was another factor conducive to farm profitability, since market prices are considerably higher than state procurement prices. Moreover, recently it was announced that farms could be eligible to receive hard currency for above-plan production, which can be dispensed as the farm sees fit. It is hoped that a combination of these measures will make profitability a realistic goal for most farms to reach.

But in the event that it is not, and officials concede that not all farms in their current format are capable of operating profitably, then provisions are made for failures. In the past, unprofitable farms subsisted on an unending supply of state loans. Now loans are considerably harder to come by, and the threat of bankruptcy and disbandment is a real one. In 1988, for example, the Russian Republic agro-industrial bank refused 2,400 applications for credit, and declared 176 farms and enterprises insolvent.[43] At least according to the director of the bank, this is becoming an effective stimulant to managers to take seriously the need for cost-effective management.

What happens to bankrupt farms? This question has long plagued supporters of bankruptcy laws in the Soviet Union. The solution currently being pursued is to amalgamate them with other, more viable farms,[44] or to turn them over to industrial enterprises to be run as subsidiary enterprises. In a speech in Omsk shortly after the plenum, Yegor Ligachev, Chairman of the Central Committee's Agricultural Policy Commission, claimed that precedent had been established; since 1986 over 140 such farms (sovkhozes and kolkhozes) had been transferred.[45]

Perhaps more interesting are attempts to reorganize sovkhozes along cooperative principles. There are at least two cases of farms having been turned into a joint-stock company. Twelve organizations, among them industrial, construction, and land reclamation organs, jointly operate a cooperative sovkhoz in Vladimir oblast.[46] Shares of a greenhouse sovkhoz[47] in Lvov were sold among industrial enterprises and the workers of the farm. The profits and a portion of the produce accrue directly to the farm workers or the industrial enterprises, who then distribute them among their workers.[48]

Thus, the centralized RAPO has been abandoned (along with its powerful all-union counterpart, *Gosagroprom*), and has been replaced with a variety of management organizations which are designed to be more responsive to the needs of the farms and enterprises which make up their constituencies. At the same time the leasing program (and more recently, a homesteading, peasant-based family farming program in parts of the country) has been widely touted as a solution to both the management and incentive problems. Now it is time to turn to an analysis of why it has been necessary to change emphasis in local agricultural management policy.

The Difficulties of Organizational Reform

The question that remains, and the question this article ultimately addresses, is why Gorbachev and the adherents of perestroika have deemphasized centralized raion-level management organizations and have switched the focus to cooperative forms of management and leasing contracts. The answer lies with the difficulties of inducing change in organizational and managerial behavior quickly enough to achieve results. A commonly held opinion among both Soviets and western observers is that for perestroika to have any chance of succeeding some results must be achieved soon;[49] this is particularly the case with food products. It became apparent that even if organizational reform could succeed in increasing consumer-ready food products, such a success would not come in the immediate future, and would at best be a gradual improvement in the course of a decade or two—clearly too long for supporters of perestroika to wait.

Why has organizational reform been so unsuccessful? Why, assuming that raion-level management organs can induce more output, is it necessarily a long-term proposition? Western specialists in implementation evaluation identify a number of factors that affect the course of successful policy implementation. By analyzing such factors, and by considering certain organizational issues (particularly organizational culture and authoritative integrity), the difficulties of inducing relatively rapid managerial change at the raion level are apparent.

Policy Implementation Analysis

Policy implementation studies by Mazmanian and Sabatier and Edwards offer analytical frameworks of variables that affect the course of implementation.[50] The following five factors are adapted from those studies.[51] (1) *Policy coherence:* the analytical task is to examine the provisions of the policy to see whether they suitably address the problem; in this case it means positing the structure and rights of each organization against its responsibilities. If, with the advantage of hindsight, it is evident that the latter cannot be achieved on the basis of the former, then difficulties in implementation are the expected result. (2) *Communication:* this concerns the degree to which the center has made both the letter and the spirit of the policy package clear to all actors at the local level. (3) *Resources:* with respect to each of the raion management organizations necessary resources include staff (with, importantly, sufficient education and training), motivational incentives, and funds to achieve stated goals. (4) *Disposition:* this includes the attitude of officials and staff toward their responsibilities and the authority formally accorded to them, as well as the attitudes of officials elsewhere—in this case, farms and enterprises, and the *raikom*—which are in close contact with the raion management organizations. (5) *The bureaucratic setting:* this final factor is the milieu in which management organizations function. It includes issues of existing standard operating procedures and fragmentation of responsibilities among different organizations, but also includes the issue of the nature of the management hierarchy within which agricultural management organizations operate.

Policy Coherence

None of the raion-level organizations can possibly accomplish all the goals which are designated for them. For example, a significant part of the service problem rests with the lack of spare parts; that is a matter of central planning and investment, and is not something that can be effectively dealt with in any one raion. The transportation infrastructure is something that can only be developed gradually if left to local funds, and it depends on the allocation of construction materials, which is also a matter of central planning. Yet, despite the fact that many factors are beyond the control of raion management organs to affect, by virtue of their structure they are at least able to provide the necessary organizational linkages to greatly improve coordination among raion food enterprises. Yet evidence indicates that coordination is often still lacking. The problem, then, is not so much with the formal structure of these organs (adequately designed in these cases) as it is with other factors.

Communication

Communication of both the letter and spirit of each management program is not a problem. With the resources the center can muster in the field of communications—official documents, newspapers, specialized journals, and the channels of policy dissemination through both the ministerial hierarchy and the party—local-level officials are not left wondering what the rights and responsibilities of each organization are. Therefore, adequate communication exists, and cannot account for the lack of effectiveness of these organizations.

Organizational Resources

While some of the needs for organizational resources are met in each case (particularly staff numbers, incentive bonuses, and organizational finances), one crucial one is lacking. Education and training levels in many cases are either not sufficient or are poorly conceived. This is the case not only with the officials and staffers of the management organizations themselves, but also with the most important officials with which they must regularly interact—farm personnel, farm workers, party officials. While many managers, staffers, and officials have higher education degrees, many do not. When they do have advanced education or training, it is relatively rarely concentrated in management. A few statistics gleaned from the press and interviews illustrate the problem:

• One article claimed that only 7.3 percent of all farm and enterprise chairmen had a formal education in economics.[52]

• In the Ukraine, one of the most important agricultural regions in the country, estimates indicate that less than 50 percent of farm staffers in key positions in finance and bookkeeping have advanced training.[53]

• In outlying areas the figures are worse. One researcher claimed that in the whole of Siberia and the Far East, there are only enough specialists with higher education degrees in either management or an agricultural specialty to allot one to every five farms each year.[54]

• One example of the difficulty of implementing policy is the introduction of collective contracts, a program for which raion management organizations are partially responsible. Many farm officials do not understand the details of how to introduce the contracts; many more do not know how to execute them. The worst figures come from provincial areas. By early 1988 (several years after the collective contract was first introduced), in the Altai krai in southern Siberia, only 3 percent of all farms had fully introduced it. In Kirgizia, in Central Asia, contracts were introduced among sheep farms, but after three or four months they existed only on paper because no one understood how they were to work.[55]

• Many of the higher education degrees held by both raion and farm officials are in agronomy, animal husbandry, or engineering. Management science is a new specialty. Thus those with higher education often have no management skills or training in financial and economic matters. Even raion-level officials do not always understand basic precepts of economic management. A report from Azerbaijan on the RAPO claimed the following:

> The lack of knowledge on the part of RAPO chairmen and specialists of the essence of such concrete economic categories as profitability, cost of production, price, [and] return on investment . . . discredits the very idea of *khozraschet* [in essence, undermines agricultural perestroika].[56]

The last problem has been addressed somewhat in the press. For example, in mid-1987, *Pravda* ran an article discussing delegation of authority.[57] More importantly, some educational institutions have begun to emphasize management training. One of the vice-chairmen of Gosagroprom stated that priorities in education of farm management personnel were being changed to emphasize skills in accountability and management in order to promote economic independence.[58] In addition to re-orienting training of future managers now in higher education, many farm, RAPO, and oblast officials are undergoing retraining. Gosagroprom operates a specialized school, the *Vysshaia shkola,* at the Timeriazev Agricultural Academy in Moscow for oblast and raion officials, who attend for two weeks and hear lectures about the *khoziastvennyi* mechanism, cost-accounting *(khozraschet)*, and self-financing. Similar schools operate for RAPO and farm officials in Stavropol,[59] serving Stavropol krai, and at the Lenin Agricultural Academy's Siberian branch near Novosibirsk, for Western Siberia. In the Belorussian republic, a special school trains chairmen and directors of unprofitable and low-profit farms.[60] It is by this method that agricultural managers are gradually being retrained in the spirit of perestroika, according to "economic methods of management."[61]

Current education levels, as well as traditional emphases on technical training at the expense of management training, provide a significant hindrance to the effectiveness of raion management organizations. Changes in management style may not happen until both the level and character of education change. An oblast party first secretary in the Ukraine claimed that improvements in management and labor policies depend precisely on raising education levels.[62] Another specialist has made the same argument; until officials and specialists of all levels from the center down to the collectives become skilled in new methods of management they will continue to fall back on crude command styles of management *(administrirovanie)*.[63] But while this problem has been recognized, the tandem processes of training more graduates in management skills and retraining existing managers promise to be slow in forthcoming.

Disposition

The matter of the disposition of local officials to raion management organizations is an important factor. It is not only the disposition of the raion officials toward their own positions and mandate, but the disposition of farm and enterprise chairmen, raion party officials, and officials higher in the agricultural management hierarchy.

It is at this point that one of the advantages of each of these new organizations should come into play—the very fact that they are new.[64] Officials of each of the management organizations have a clearly stated mandate, exhortations from central authorities to assert their authority, the incentive of financial bonuses and, theoretically, career advancement if their organization succeeds in becoming authoritative and fulfills its mandate. Yet, often these officials are either unwilling to assert their legal authority or unwilling to use it properly. Why would they ignore their legally stated mandate, financial incentives, and apparent career enhancement by seemingly rejecting the essence of the raion management organizations?

First, it must be argued that the purported advantages of being a new organization do not necessarily exist in the Soviet Union. It is arguably impossible for a new organization to avoid adapting to the existing organizational culture of state bodies. One of the endemic characteristics of state officials is deference both to officials of higher standing organs and to party counterparts. Any new organization draws personnel from existing organizations, and with these personnel comes the nearly automatic proclivity to defer. This proclivity develops into an important element of the culture of the organization, incontrovertibly undermining its effectiveness as a management body. Secondly, career advancement is still heavily influenced by the *nomenklatura* process (which is to say by party officials) and has no necessary correlation to performance. Therefore, independence in decision making, which is often not likely to ingratiate oneself with the corresponding party officials, is not an expected result.

Thus, raion management officials are often not disposed to use their authority and party officials are likewise not disposed to encourage them to use it. Changing the disposition of party officials is an ongoing process, but as with managers, an extended one as well. Articles appear regularly in party media such as *Pravda, Kommunist,* and *Partiinaia zhizn'*, as well as the agricultural daily *Sel'skaia zhizn'*, discussing the role of party officials and the style by which they should carry out their tasks. Much of the 19th Party Conference in mid-1988 was devoted to clearly defining the role of the party and even discussing possible legal limitations on party power. Evidence indicates, however, that no new attitude of concession has appeared yet among local party officials. The same argument can be made regarding oblast officials. Used to authority unchallenged from below, they show little willingness not to assert their authority, legally based or not.

The factors of education and disposition are related. In cases where party and/or raion management officials continue to adhere to the sole priority of plan fulfillment, they are much more likely to ignore the spirit of the reforms. *Raikom* officials will not concede authority to the management organizations; and the latter will not concede independence to farms and enterprises. As both sets of officials understand the changing priorities at the center, there is at least a chance that they will accept and support them.

But this leads to a different problem. Perestroika is a process barely under way. While agricultural reforms preceded broad economic and political reforms by several years, it was with the advent of perestroika in 1985 that central support for local decision making grew the strongest. But with the advent of perestroika another phenomenon arose; local officials in both party and state bodies did not and in many cases still have not fully committed themselves to perestroika. In the case of party officials it may be based in part on fear of losing power, but in any case there is a certain amount of skepticism that perestroika will last. Until local officials gain confidence that perestroika will succeed, and that there will be no sudden end to it as part of a conservative backlash, they will be hesitant to fully identify themselves with it. They often try to occupy a position that is not fully for perestroika, while at the same time not against it, hedging their bets until the political landscape is more discernible. Since much of the success of the raion management organizations, as with many of the facets of perestroika, depends on local officials taking initiative in addressing long-standing problems, the tendency toward riding the fence is not conducive to organizational successes. Paradoxically, while raion management organizations were strongly supported by the reform leadership with the advent of perestroika, the uncertainty in the political realm caused by perestroika also works to their detriment.

The Bureaucratic Setting:
Intra-organizational Factors

Two intra-organizational factors account for some of the difficulties in managing the raion food economy. The first has to do with a distinction between centrally passed laws and existing intra-organizational regulations and procedures. Centrally passed laws define broad policy and programs; how each agency implements those policies and programs into actual day-to-day operations depends on internal procedures developed in accord with pre-existing policy. As policy changes, these too need to change, but the time required to change internal standard operating procedures and regulations can be extensive.

The issue of farm independence provides a good example. It has been a goal for three decades,[65] but it has proven difficult to achieve. One obvious reason is the command decision-making style noted above. But the problems with farm independence are more complicated. For a long time one of the main barriers standing in the way of farm independence was the lack of technical competence on the part of its management; while this is still a problem it is more often in areas of finance and accounting than in matters of agronomy and animal husbandry. However, regulations still exist in republic and oblast-level agro-industrial committees stipulating in minute detail how farms are to be run. Such stipulations include the number of workers that should be applied to a certain herd size of milking cows, the proper ratio of land devoted to feed crops (irrespective of yield), the number of livestock, what times and how many times a day livestock should be fed, the assortment of vegetable crops that must be maintained, and so on. Any Soviet specialist today will argue that these matters are best left to the farm management; this is indeed the intent of current policy. But regulations still exist on the books, and it is not a simple matter to root them out and eliminate them. One republic agro-industrial committee official told how he had a committee that worked on just that matter. Any existing regulation on a matter that they determined could be effectively and better handled by farm management was eliminated. But the process was slow going, and until official notification was given many directors felt obliged to comply with them. Similarly, many raion officials feel obligated to enforce them, either because they are accustomed to enforcing regulations from above or because they fear disciplinary action if they do not.[66]

Similar regulations hamper the ability of departments within Gosagroprom to work together, which complicates matters at the level of the raion. Each department has a host of existing regulations and procedures dating from the time when they were separate ministries; these can interfere with the rights and responsibilities of raion management organizations. The RAPO's centralized funds provide an example. Some processing plants still resist contributing to the funds because their disbursements are carefully controlled by intra-organizational regulations that have not caught up with the reforms.[67] Construction and machinery repair organizations still work according to seasonal timetables determined when these organizations were independent; such timetables do not work to the benefit of farms. Yet the service organizations tended to feel more beholden to such regulations than they did to the authority of the RAPO, their immediate superior in the organizational hierarchy.[68] Revamping existing regulations and eliminating or replacing those which work contrary to the intent of reform is, once again, a gradual process.

A second intra-organizational set of relationships having to do with the system of middle level organizations formed in the late sixties and seventies in order to induce specialization and technical advancement has not been entirely dismantled. Many specialized organizations were formed at the oblast, krai, and republic level to deal exclusively with one or another variant of agricultural service, production, and/or processing. For example, *ptitsepromy* were organizations that supervised contracts between hatcheries, farms that produced eggs or cooking chickens, and plants that processed poultry. *Plemob"edineniia* were similar organizations that included breeding lots, farms with feedlots for fattening cattle, and meat-packing plants. *Agropromstroi* was a supervisory organ for construction, which included enterprises within the *Minselstroi* (rural construction ministry) system, the Interkolkhoz construction organizations, and even the construction departments of some farms and enterprises. The purpose for these and other similar organizations was to encourage coordination among organizations all involved in one stage or another of production of the same product (or provision of a service), and to make new methods and techniques readily available to farm and enterprise workers and managers. The formation of such trusts and production associations (POs), as they were called, was a useful supplement to the splintered ministerial system in which the agricultural economy was organized, but proved unable to overcome ministerial boundaries and usually ended up as no more than a subdivision of one of the ministries.

Oddly enough, many of these organizations still exist, never having been formally dismantled. Their coordinative function, which they never really succeeded in fulfilling, was replaced by the RAPO (and since then, by the *agrokombinat* or agro-association) and oblast, krai, and republic agro-industrial committees. Their scientific function (development and introduction of advanced techniques) has been taken over by a newer organization dedicated exclusively to that task (the NPO).[69] Although no clear rationale exists for their continued existence, many remain. Considering that they were originally formed to help achieve coordination, it is ironic that they are now cited as obstacles in effective coordination. Yet one official in construction planning in Arkhangelsk oblast claims that while raion construction organs were formally included within the RAPO's composition, they were in practice beholden to the oblast *agropromstroi*, a trust that existed side-by-side with the construction department of the oblast agro-industrial organ, both of which had the same responsibilities.[70] Yet the ties that existed from prior to 1986, when raion construction organs were subordinate directly to the *agropromstroi* trust, are stronger than the more recent raion management organizations. If the oblast agro-industrial committee could not overcome such ties, raion organizations could hardly be expected to, and consequently they were in no position to supervise relations between construction organs and their clients (primarily farms). Similarly, a *raikom* secretary in Chita oblast claimed that the RAPO in his raion had not succeeded in becoming an authoritative organ that could fulfill its designated responsibilities, and blamed that fact on the continued ties between many of the farms and processing enterprises and oblast-level trusts and production associations.[71]

Thus formal reorganization, while a significant step in itself, is only part of the process of organizational reform, and it is the easiest as well. Changing or eliminating regulations and behavioral patterns of different agencies of the management hierarchy is a long-term process. It, too, links up with the issue of education and professional skills. Leading a change in behavioral habits and supervising an overhaul of bureaucratic regulations as extensive as those in the agricultural management hierarchy require considerably more management and administrative skills than supervising a static situation in which rules and procedures are standardized and staffers are well acquainted with them and with their positions within the organization. Soviet bureaucracy is not known for its innovative or dynamic character; indeed, one of the most pervasive characteristics of the legacy of Stalinism is the disinclination, even aversion, to initiative on the part of bureaucrats and managers.

The Bureaucratic Setting: Overlapping Responsibility

A final factor is the notion of fragmentation, a situation in which multiple organizations are given responsibilities in the same implementation process. The cases of the parallel *agropromstroi* and the construction department of the oblast agro-industrial committee in Arkhangelsk oblast is a close approximation of fragmentation. The idea is that of two or more implementing agencies (or in this case, management organizations) given responsibility for different jurisdictions or different stages in the same management process, in which they would nominally complement each other. The problem arises when the different agencies have no incentive to cooperate with one another. The Arkhangelsk example is simple and complete duplication of responsibility, a type of fragmentation that can only be counterproductive.

Another, more subtle form of fragmentation exists. It is the overlapping responsibility of *raikom* and management officials. Formally, no such overlap exists; through carefully crafted policy and propaganda the responsibilities of each are clear and distinct from one another. But the center sends signals to lower levels that conflict with the official line. The ultimate success of the agricultural sector is as much the responsibility of party officials as it is of state (including raion management) officials. This is not new; a 1970 resolution criticizing the Meat and Dairy Ministry's party organization for the ministry's performance is a typical example.[72] The situation has not changed. A *Radio Moscow* report in spring 1986 noted that two oblast party committee first secretaries were severely criticized for "failure to provide livestock farms in their areas with adequate quantities of high quality fodder." Moreover, they were to be held "personally responsible" for correcting the problems.[73] The report of RAPO officials in Azerbaijan who did not understand basic economic concepts went on to place primary blame on three party secretaries.[74] Central Committee resolutions on the inadequacy of animal husbandry in Cheliabinsk oblast and farming in Rostov oblast held party officials as responsible as their counterpart state officials.[75] Thus, while raion party secretaries are directed to conceded day-to-day management of the raion food economy to management organizations such as the RAPO, the *agrokombinat*, the agrofirm, and the agro-association, they receive the clear message from above that they can be held personally responsible for failures. The latter message is a strong inducement to become heavily involved in economic management to ensure success, defined in the very least as plan fulfillment and, more recently, profitable operation of each farm and enterprise. While party officials can be criticized for interference, they rarely lose their jobs over it, but some have lost their positions for economic failures in their constituency. The incentive to intervene in such cases may be stronger than the incentive to concede, especially if managers appear to be incompetent or otherwise incapable of effectively managing. As long as both party and management officials are held responsible for the productivity of the raion food economy, this situation is likely to continue. And as long as the *raikom* holds the primary level of power, control of appointments and promotions (including that of management officials), the *raikom* will prevail in any matter of intervention.

Thus, a number of factors pertaining to the environment in which raion management organizations function work to their disadvantage, and are beyond the capacity of management officials to change. They can do little about counterproductive standard operating procedures and regulations; the same is true of having to deal with unneeded but powerful, higher-level management organizations. And local management officials can do no more about the Soviet party-state relationship than the local soviets, industrial enterprises, and research institutions can, all of which have faced the same problem of party intrusion for years. In such an environment, the effectiveness of local management organizations can only be compromised.

Conclusion

The difficulties encountered by central authorities in trying to form and develop raion agricultural management organizations and implement attending policies can be attributed primarily to three problems: the level and character of education of local officials, their disposition toward the spirit of localized management, and the nature of the bureaucratic setting within which local management organizations operate. Many local officials do not have higher education; when they do, it is often in a technical discipline with little or no management training. The adaptation of local management organizations to (or adoption of) the persisting organizational culture of state organizations, which calls for deference to higher-standing authorities as well as to party officials, has undermined one of the central elements of effective local management: independent decision making according to "economic methods of management." The general uncertainty caused by perestroika has induced many local officials—including those of the Party committees, the management organizations (particularly the RAPO), and farms and enterprises—to adopt a "wait and see" attitude, further undermining the initiative necessary to overcome perceived risks in making decisions in agricultural management.

Other factors are involved. Arturo Israel, associated with the World Bank, argues in his study of implementation of development projects that the presence of competition can greatly induce a more favorable disposition among implementing officials.[76] Competition could theoretically result from service enterprises that vie with one another for contracts, for instance, or an American-style dealer system of equipment and spare parts distribution. A similar result could come from competition among politicians and bureaucrats, perhaps because of overlapping jurisdictions or competitive selection based on some measure of competence. But neither type of competition exists in the Soviet Union; bureaucratic control of prices and ministerial monopoly of economic groups prevents any such competition. The absence of competition thus removes one theoretical inducement to competent and judicious action on the part of implementing officials. A competition surrogate, Israel argues, would be the presence of strong willed politicians who have a personal investment in the fulfillment of a policy. As argued above, however, the opposite is the case; most authorities are at best ambivalent about the RAPO and similar policy programs.

A second factor, offered by Glynn Cochrane (another World Bank analyst), is the scale of implementation.[77] The smaller the scale of implementation, he argues, the more likely the policy will be effectively implemented. The attention of central authorities is in such cases more focused and the problem is more "tractable," to use Mazmanian and Sabatier's term. Evidence from the RAPO program nominally supports this thesis; while the RAPO was still confined to primarily Latvia and Estonia prior to its countrywide introduction, it functioned much better than its post-1982 performance. Latvia and Estonia are two of the smallest republics and the number of RAPOs between the two numbered no more than forty-five. Ultimately, there were over 3,000 RAPOs countrywide. The difference in scale is self-evident. Yet, while acknowledging this factor, it must be noted that educational levels among Latvians and Estonians are much higher than the norm, and prior to 1982 the RAPO was still a fledgling program which both republics claimed to be their own. The stakes of local and republic officials in the success of the RAPO were consequently higher.

Thus, even if the Soviet leadership were to maintain faith in centralized agricultural management at the local level, it is forced to concede that results reaped from such an approach are going to be long in coming. And as noted, before, the pro-perestroika leadership cannot afford the luxury of a gradual improvement in production and output. They will most certainly continue to try to rationalize management structure and process in order to reduce losses, but have realized that increased production within existing or reformed managerial structures is unlikely in the near term. The only alternative is to decentralize further. That is currently being done in two ways. The first is by bypassing most levels of the managerial hierarchy and focusing on the individual or group and relying on direct incentives. The leasing contracts, an attempt to once again "make the peasant the master of the land," are intended to do just that. The second is to form management organizations which are responsive to constituent (farms and enterprises) needs. That is the overall thrust of the *agrokombinat*, the agrofirm and the agro-association, all of which are intended to operate on the cooperative principle.

Notes

1. Funds for the research from which this paper developed were originally provided by a Zahm Travel Grant from the University of Notre Dame and the Kellogg Institute for International Studies Seed Money Fund, and subsequently, the International Research and Exchanges Board (IREX) and the Soviet Ministry of Higher Education, which supported seven months of field research in the Soviet Union. Support was also provided by the University of Illinois Summer Research Laboratory, the Zentrum für Kontinentale Agrar.-und Wirtschaftsforschung in Giessen, West Germany, and the Institut für Weltwirtschaft in Kiel, West Germany. I am also indebted to Claude Phillips and Werner Hahn for very helpful comments on various drafts.

2. For example, the November 1987 Revolution Day speech by Gorbachev that was to set the tone for discussions about the Stalinist heritage was considerably more muted than preliminary indications. Another example, to be discussed later in this article, is the March 1989 Plenum on agricultural policy which was less radical than many, including Gorbachev, had let on in the preceding months. Both of these events represent cases of compromise, indicating the balance of power among elite policy-makers.

3. This article will barely address the leasing program, as it is discussed in considerable depth elsewhere in this issue.

4. The local administrative district in the Soviet Union is the *raion*, which is the term that will be used in this article.

5. An *oblast* is the administrative territory that corresponds most closely to a province or state. Each oblast may contain from 12 to 30 raions.

6. *Raionnoe agropromyshlennoe ob"edinenie.*

7. *Planovoe khoziaistvo*, 7 (July 1978): 44–55; *Sovetskaia Rossiia* (April 25, 1981): 1; *Sotsialisticheskaia industriia* (April 9, 1982): 3; *Ekonomicheskaia gazeta*, no. 21 (1978): 11; no. 31 (1987): 15.

8. *Pravda*, November 23, 1985.

9. *Kommunist* 4 (April 1984): 18–26.

10. *Izvestiia* (January 23, 1987): 2; (December 23, 1987): 2; *Sel'skaia zhizn'* (January 22, 1988): 1.

11. *Sel'skaia zhizn'* (January 5, 1988): 2; (January 16, 1988): 2; (April 22, 1988): 1.

12. *Pravda* (December 5, 1986): 2; (January 25, 1987): 1–2.

13. *Penzenskaia pravda* (August 28, 1986): 2; *Pravda* (September 15, 1987): 2; *Ekonomicheskaia gazeta* 48, no. 2 (1987): 9–11; *Sel'skaia zhizn'* (December 4, 1987): 2; (May 8, 1988): 1.

14. *Ekonomicheskaia gazeta*, no. 21 (1987): 11; *Sel'skaia zhizn'* (February 10, 1988): 2.

15. Author's interviews, 1987.

16. *Pravda* (September 25, 1987): 2.

17. *Ekonomicheskaia gazeta* 48, no. 2 (1987): 9–11.

18. *Sel'skaia zhizn'* (June 29, 1988): 2–7; (June 30, 1988): 1–3.

19. *Sel'skaia zhizn'* (March 16, 1989): 3.

20. A *krai* is similar to an *oblast*.

21. *Agropromyshlennyi kombinat "Kuban'."* Moscow: Agropromizdat, 1986.

22. *FBIS Daily Reports,* September 16, R1–10, and 19, 1986, R1–2.

23. *Ekonomicheskaia gazeta*, no. 44 (1986): 12–13; no. 49 (1986): 10–11.

24. *FBIS Daily Report,* August 10, R1–11; and 11, 1987, R1–23.

25. Author's interviews, 1987; *Ekonomicheskaia gazeta*, no. 21 (1987):11; no. 49 (1987): 11; no. 48 (1987): 18; *Sel'skaia zhizn'* (December 1, 1987): 1; (March 10, 1988): 1; (April 22, 1988): 2; (May 18, 1988): 2; (October 1988): 1; (October 13, 1988): 2.

26. Adazhi is in a highly unusual and envious position in that its fur production allows it opportunities unavailable to other such enterprises. It sells furs at the Leningrad fur auction twice a year, reaping thousands of rubles in hard currency profits. While not allowed to keep all the hard currency, it has been able to purchase French machinery for making the potato sticks and has other hard currency purchases planned. Information gained from interviews at Adazhi and Kalnyn'sh (1987). In addition, in winter 1989 farm management officials visited the Kellogg offices in Battle Creek, Michigan, to discuss the purchase of technologies for making American-style breakfast cereals, including corn flakes.

27. Author's interview, 1987; *Kommunist Sovetskoi Latvii*, no. 12 (1986): 22–27; *Sel'skaia zhizn'* (September 21, 1988): 1; (September 16, 1988): 2; (September 30, 1988): 2.

28. *Ekonomicheskaia gazeta*, no. 34 (1987): 6–7.

29. *FBIS Daily Report: Soviet Union,* February 24, R17–20, and 25, R5–22, 1987.

30. *Sel'skaia zhizn'* (September 21, 1988): 1.

31. *Sel'skaia zhizn'* (October 16, 1988): 1.

32. *FBIS Daily Report: Soviet Union,* November 10, 1987, 80.

33. *Sel'skaia zhizn'* (May 22, 1988): 2.

34. *Sel'skaia zhizn'* (November 24, 1987): 2.

35. *Ekonomicheskaia gazeta*, no. 48 (1987): 9.

36. *FBIS Daily Report: Soviet Union,* November 10, 1987, 80.

37. Nikonov lost his position with the high-level personnel changes during the October 1989 Plenum.

38. *Sel'skaia zhizn'* (February 7, 1989): 1. This figure was also given by Gorbachev at the plenum, but he claimed that it included 110 agro-associations of the *Novomoskovskoe* type. *Sel'skaia zhizn'* (March 16, 1989): 3.

39. *Vestnik Agroproma,* 13 (March 1989): 6.

40. Gorbachev refers to this discussion in his speech to the March 1989 Plenum. *Sel'skaia zhizn'* (March 16, 1989): 2.

41. Ibid.

42. Author's interviews, 1986–87.

43. *Sel'skaia zhizn'* (April 15, 1989): 1–2.

44. Noted by Gorbachev at the March 1989 Plenum. *Sel'skaia zhizn'* (March 16, 1989): 3.

45. *Sel'skaia zhizn'* (April 2, 1989): 2.

46. *Sel'skaia zhizn'* (February 7, 1989): 1.

47. About 4 percent of vegetables are grown in huge greenhouse complexes that can be found on the outskirts of most large cities. *Sel'skaia zhizn'* (February 7, 1989): 2.

48. Ibid.

49. Note, for example, Marshall Goldman's *Gorbachev's Challenge* (New York: Norton, 1988).

50. Daniel Mazmanian and Paul Sabatier, "The Implementation of Public Policy: A Framework of Analysis," in Mazmanian and Sabatier (eds.), *Effective Policy Implementation* (Lexington, MA: Lexington Books, 1981); and George Edwards III, *Implementing Public Policy* (Washington, DC: Congressional Quarterly Press, 1980).

51. The foregoing analysis is considerably more developed in chapter 4 of the author's study of the RAPO. Jim Butterfield, *Soviet Local Agriculture and the RAPO Reform* (Ph.D. dissertation, University of Notre Dame, 1988).

52. *Sel'skaia zhizn'* (April 27, 1988): 2.

53. *Ekonomicheskaia gazeta,* no. 20 (1984): 6.

54. Author's interview, 1987.

55. *Ekonomicheskaia gazeta,* no. 35 (1987): 10.

56. *Sel'skaia zhizn'* (January 15, 1988): 3.

57. *Pravda* (June 1, 1987): 2.

58. *Sel'skaia zhizn'* (April 27, 1988): 2.

59. Ibid.

60. Ibid.

61. "Economic methods of management" are management according to principles of cost-accounting, efficient utilization of resources, quality-consciousness, and, as always, plan fulfillment.

62. *Ekonomicheskaia gazeta,* no. 20 (1984): 6.

63. *Pravda* (June 2, 1987): 2.

64. Some of the following argument was made in the author's "Raion agroindustrial associations in Soviet agriculture," in Wadekin, Laird and Grossman (eds.), *Communist Agriculture* (London: Routledge, forthcoming).

65. Karl Eugen Wadekin, *Agrarian Policies in Communist Europe* (Totowa, NJ: Allenheld, Osmun and Co., 1982), pp. 53–55.

66. Author's interview.

67. Author's interview.

68. Author's interview.

69. *Nauchno-proizvodstvennoe ob"edinenie.*

70. *Sel'skaia zhizn'* (January 22, 1988): 1.

71. *Sel'skaia zhizn'* (January 8, 1988): 2.

72. *Partiinaia zhizn'*, no. 4 (April 1970): 3–6.

73. Dawn Mann, "Party secretaries made personally responsible for agricultural failings," *Radio Liberty Research* 236/86 (June 24, 1986).

74. *Sel'skaia zhizn'* (January 15, 1988): 3.

75. *Sel'skaia zhizn'* (December 4, 1987): 1; (February 25, 1988): 1. In another case, this one dealing with social services in rural villages, party officials in Kurgan were held exclusively responsible for failures. *Sel'skaia zhizn'* (May 20, 1988): 1.

76. Arturo Israel, *Institutional Development: Incentives to Performance* (Baltimore: Johns Hopkins University Press, 1987), pp. 89–106.

77. Glynn Cochrane, *Reforming National Institutions for Economic Development* (Boulder, CO: Westview Press, 1986). Cochrane refers to this as the size of the target population affected by the policy.

Edward C. Cook

Reforming Soviet Agriculture
Problems with Farm Finances
and Equity Considerations

Agriculture is in the most dire financial straits of any major sector of
the Soviet economy. Agriculture could well be considered the Soviet
Union's savings and loan crisis. A strange combination of inappropriate administrative regulation and a lack of accountability for the use of
funds has led to a tremendous amount of bad debt, requiring costly
government bailouts. The financial morass and the continued sluggish
growth in production have centered attention on the need to restructure
the agricultural sector. Though the impetus for change is there, agricultural finances are also complicating efforts at restructuring. The state
can ill afford to write off the roughly 70 billion rubles of postponed
credit in the agro-industrial complex (60 billion of which is in agriculture itself). How these liabilities might be transferred through a restructuring remains uncertain.

The deteriorating macroeconomic situation is having the same
two-sided influence. While the need for a significant supply-side
response for agricultural commodities increases, shortages throughout the system lead the state to revert to administrative controls.
Hoped-for diversification of linkages, integration, and rationalization
is not taking place because of state price regulation and other methods of state control of resource flows, and barriers to alternative
ownership forms.

Uncertainty remains among policymakers as to just how radical a
restructuring is necessary or desirable. There is far from a consensus
on such central issues as land tenure, ownership of capital, and the
system of price formation. The cause of the discord is not simply
continued disagreement about the proper place of administrative con-

The author is affiliated with the Economic Research Service of the U.S. Department of Agriculture. The views expressed in this paper are his own and not
necessarily those of the department or the U.S. government.

trol, but equity considerations which have become ingrained in Soviet agriculture since the mid-1960s.

The Brezhnev period saw the initiation of a massive modernization effort in agriculture characterized by essentially arbitrary resource allocation decisions and ill-advised financial policies. From the state's side, wage payments in agriculture were guaranteed at a certain level and bailouts were offered to avert farm bankruptcy. In return, the state assumed that sub-par farms would utilize its largesse to draw their performance up to an average level. Needless to say, laggard farms did not disappear, but in a certain sense prospered. The lack of financial discipline fostered a wide divergence among farms in terms of efficiency and financial health.

The chances of implementing a reform of real significance without having a negative impact on a large number of farms, and the workers on those farms, are seriously in doubt. (One might argue that this was not the case in China in the late 1970s.) First, the state is not in a position to smooth the transition by pumping substantially more resources into agriculture, which is something the Chinese did.[1] Second, many Soviet analysts complain that the peasant has largely been erased from the countryside, replaced by the disinterested farm worker. The logic of the more radical restructuring programs calls for the pre-eminence of the peasant rather than the farm worker. Third, as will be shown below, a significant share of Soviet farms are subsidized by the state to such an extent that even a highly effective restructuring in terms of efficiency will leave them worse off if their subsidies are eliminated.

The continued discord on important reform issues means that no comprehensive, systemic approach to reform has been possible. The first part of this paper looks at major financial aspects of Soviet agriculture. They are important elements in the current restructuring in their own right. In addition, financial programs have been the conduits for the major equity policies of recent decades. The second part of this paper looks at current discussion of some important reform issues. The final section offers some observation on the future.

The Financial Crisis in Soviet Agriculture

Table 1, which provides data on end-of-year outstanding debt owed by state and collective farms, shows the mounting burden of the state's

Table 1. Debt Outstanding,
Collective and State Farms and
Interfarm Enterprises, End of Year

	Short-term	Long-term (billion rubles)	Total
1970	8.6	10.8	19.4
1975	25.5	22.9	48.4
1980	57.6	42.4	100.0
1983	70.8	53.0	123.8
1984	76.3	55.2	131.5
1985	82.3	57.1	139.4
1986	84.5	60.2	144.7
1987	87.0	61.0	148.0

Source: *Narodnoe khoziaistvo v 1985 godu*, p. 566; *Narodnoe khoziaistvo v 1987 godu*, p. 595.

generosity in the countryside. A growing amount of credit, in and of itself, is not a bad thing. But in this case, a sizeable portion of state and collective farms (about two-thirds of all collective farms) cannot cover their short-term loans from current gross income (Petrov 1989). For one-third of all Soviet farms the problem is particularly severe, with 22 billion rubles in short-term loans unrepayable and carried over from year to year (Petrov 1989). In some cases these short-term loans are converted to long-term credit. Virtually all outstanding long-term farm debt (roughly 60 billion rubles) has been postponed for repayment during 1990–2005. For the vast majority of these credits, interest payments have also been postponed (Obozintsev 1988). The decade of the 1980s witnessed a continuing series of these postponements, creating a growing debt overhang in agriculture. For collective farms, the amount of postponed debt nearly doubled between 1983 and 1988 (Puchkova 1988, Semenov 1989). For the entire agro-industrial complex, postponed debt now totals at least 68 billion rubles, of which 58 billion is owed by collective and state farms (Semenov 1989).

At this point, there is little reason to suspect that these debts will be repaid without further concessional steps by the government. A best-case scenario for the future includes a significant burst in production efficiency by Soviet farms, which would lower production costs and raise net farm income. Another possible outcome is further increases in state subsidies to agriculture to bolster net farm income. Significantly rapid inflation could shrink the real value of the debts and facilitate repayment. Possibly the most likely outcome is that these debts will eventually be written off. Only the first of these scenarios avoids a sizeable loss to an already strained state budget.

In the United States such a financial crisis in agriculture would result in restructuring, and farmers themselves would bear a large share of the costs. In the case of the savings and loan crisis, the government is obligated to back up deposit insurance guarantees and will wind up bearing most of the cost of restructuring. For the USSR agricultural sector, implicit social guarantees are forcing the state to assume the costs of the crisis. What's more, these guarantees are complicating attempts to restructure. During the 1980s increased subsidies and debt write-off were the methods used to deal with the growing financial problem. Introduction of the Food Program in 1983 allowed farms in particularly difficult financial positions to write off nearly 10 billion rubles in debts. Increases in agricultural subsidies during the 1980s allowed farm profits to increase from virtually nil in 1982 to over 30 billion rubles in 1988. These policies have been costly and have not addressed the underlying systemic causes of inefficiency.

Evidence suggests that the net drain on the state budget from the agro-industrial complex has increased by even more than subsidies over this period, due to declining budgetary revenues from vodka sales and little increase in profit taxes from related state industries. Rough estimates indicate that the relationship of the state budget to the agro-industrial complex was in balance as recently as 1982, but that since that time net payments from the budget have grown to the range of 40–50 billion rubles (Cook 1988).

Inefficient Investment Allocation
and the Minimum/Maximum Wage

The financial dilemma of Soviet agriculture in the 1980s has immediate roots in the investment boom in agriculture which began in the mid-1960s. It is the end result of the drive to modernize Soviet agriculture over the last 25 years, a drive which proved to be particularly

Table 2. Budgetary Subsidies to the Agro-Industrial Complex 1982-90

Category	1982	1983	1986	1987	1989 plan	1990 plan
			(billion rubles)			
Price subsidies*	29.9	54.6	63.2	64.9	55.6	61.9
Differential price bonuses	-	-	-	-	32.2	33.1
Input subsidies	8.2	4.2	5.5	5.8	-	-
Investment subsidies	32.3	33.3	26.4	28.1	20.6	21.5
Total	70.4	92.1	95.1	98.8	108.8	116.5

*For 1983-87 these include differential bonuses for financially weak farms.

Sources: V. N. Semenov, *Finansovo-kreditnyi mekhanizm v rasvitii sel'skogo khoziaistva* (Moscow: Finansy i statistika, 1983), pp. 178-83; *Prodovol'stvennaya programma i finansy* (Moscow: Finansy i statistika, 1985), p. 113; " Khozrashchet i samofinansirovanie," *APK: Ekonomika, upravlenie*, No. 3, 1989, p. 12, and " Tseny i finansy APK," *Finansy SSSR*, No. 9, 1989, pp. 19, 21.

inefficient. Financial control over resource allocation under Brezhnev became so lax as to be meaningless.

Credit and direct budgetary allocations were utilized extensively to insure that predetermined physical investment plans, such as the program for the Non-Black Soil Zone, were carried out. As the ill-coordinated mechanization and modernization process moved forward, and in combination with what was essentially a free (though administratively controlled) money policy on the part of the state, costs of production in Soviet agriculture entered a strong growth phase.

Costs did not increase equally for all farms, however. The lack of financial discipline allowed for the development of a wide disparity in farm performance. By the early 1980s, the practice of redirecting re-

Table 3. Gross Income and Labor Remuneration per Worker by Farm Profitability, Collective Farms, 1984

		Profitability level[a]			
	Negative	0-5%	5-10% (rubles)	10-15%	15-25%
Gross farm income per worker	1265	1890	2075	2275	2598
Remuneration per worker[b]	1800	1632	1631	1608	1656

[a]Profit divided by prime costs of production.
[b]Wages plus bonuses.

sources from low-cost to high-cost farms through the use of centralized funds was supplemented by the introduction of differential bonus payments for low-profit and unprofitable farms. The rationale behind these payments was that lagging farms only needed sufficient resources to bring their performance up to par. Inherent in this approach was the notion that despite past performance all farms had a right to develop further. The obvious disincentive effects of the differential bonuses apparently escaped Soviet policymakers early on, but are clear in the data in Tables 3 and 4.

The point here is not whether actual living standards are higher, lower, or the same on non-profitable compared to profitable farms, but whether there is incentive from the workers' point of view to improve performance on any farm. Not only is there evidence of a minimum wage for collective farms stemming from guarantees introduced in the mid-sixties, but also of a "maximum" wage that is not much higher. (This is not to say that individual farms in these groups do not have average wages that may be well in excess of the averages for their group as a whole.) For the weakest farms, wage payments are nearly as large as, or actually exceed, gross income. As gross income increases, wage payments go up very slightly, while the farm's share of gross income allocated to investment increases markedly.

Over 60 percent of collective farms receive some differential bonuses, yet these bonuses have not appreciably improved the financial prospects of the weakest farms. In some cases the differential bonuses have allowed inefficient farms to achieve higher profit rates in specific

**Table 4. Share of Gross Income
Allocated to Investment Funds,
and Gross Income and Wage Payments
Per Labor Day; Collective Farms, 1984**

Farm category	Share of gross income allocated to investment	Gross income per labor day	Wage payments per labor day
		rubles	
1	unprofitable, no allocations	4.7	6.4
2	profitable, no allocations	8.2	6.1
3	0-5 percent	9.2	6.1
4	5-10 percent	9.9	6.4
5	10-15 percent	10.9	6.6
6	15-20 percent	11.6	6.8
7	20-25 percent	12.5	6.9
8	25-30 percent	13.5	6.9
9	30-35 percent	13.7	6.8
10	over 35 percent	15.6	6.6

Source: I. Suslov, " Kolkhoznaia sobstvennost': problemy razvitiia," *Voprosy ekonomiki*, no. 9 (1987): 81.

years, as the data from Voronezh Oblast indicate (Table 5). One rationale for such a pattern is that it is precisely the unprofitable farms that need the highest profit rates, so as to deal with accumulated financial problems.

Despite repeated policy calls for agricultural self-sufficiency and growth in production, under the evolved Brezhnev system efficiency was sacrificed not only as the price for administrative control, but also as a result of social and equity considerations.

Restructuring—How to Do It?

The imperative for restructuring in Soviet agriculture is strong. Growth of production remains disappointing, the drain on the state budget continues to grow, and the prospects of having to write off billions of rubles of bad debts improve. If equity considerations are valid, a number of problems are immediately apparent, however. How does one

Table 5. Influence of Differential
Bonuses on the Financial Results of
Collective Farms in Voronezh Oblast,
1984-86 Average

Farm Category	Share of Bonus in Total Payments	Farm Profitability	
		After Bonus	Before Bonus
	(percent)		
1	under 10	8	3
2	11-20	10	-5
3	21-30	16	-10
4	31-40	21	-17

Source: I. M. Surkov, and A. F. Frolov, "O metodike opredeleniia differentsirovannykh nadbavok k tsenam," *Ekonomika sel'skokhoziaistvennykh i pererabativaiushchykh predpriatii*, no. 7 (1989): 34.

insure that the new "rules of the game" that restructuring brings are fair? Farms take as their starting point the inheritance from the past, full of mistakes for which they were only partly responsible under the command-directive system. Should they be fully accountable for the past? If not, how are past mistakes adjusted for? Second, restructuring will take place under a condition of widespread shortages. With an economic pie that is growing slowly, if at all, the state cannot smooth the transition by rewarding efficiency to the extent it could if the economy were in balance and growing at a healthy pace. Punishing inefficiency becomes a more important lever. The disparity in farm performance that has been fostered by the lack of financial discipline means that the shakeout from a successful restructuring will likely be severe.

This is the point where new ideas on land tenure arrangements are supposed to bear fruit. The system of leasing land by households and other small groups is seen as a potential way out for problem farms. Existing state and collective farms could reconstitute themselves as associations of leasing cooperatives, where presumably the individual lease teams would enjoy a great degree of independence. The idea of lease teams has been championed for particular problem areas such as the Non-Black Soil Zone and Siberia.

There seems to have been little discussion of whether farms in such dire financial position, some with wage payments larger than gross income, are in fact fertile ground for conversion to lease teams. A prerequisite for successful functioning of the lease team idea is appropriate connections with efficient up- and downstream partners. Without adequately responsive input and service providers, and appropriate support for storage and marketing, the lease teams will have a hard time proving effective. The experience of Polish agriculture is instructive because it is a case where small-scale, labor-intensive, private agriculture has not generated high productivity because of the absence of support from the relevant agencies. The experience of China may be misleading as a model, given the lower technological level, greater labor intensiveness, and lower living standards associated with agriculture there. Farm workers in the USSR may not (in fact, are not) jumping at the chance to leave guaranteed wages for work under such conditions.

Farmers in the Baltics now have their sights set on re-establishing bona fide private farms. (According to Ivar Raig, a representative to the Congress of People's Deputies from Estonia, there are now nearly 5,000 private farms in the Baltic Republics.) Elsewhere, farm workers either lack the entrepreneurial motivation, or are faced with unattractive terms and conditions from the lessor to enter into leasing agreements. To this point agricultural leasing remains largely subverted to the existing state and collective farm system. Support from state and collective farms has been generally poor, prices offered are usually lower than farm-gate prices for state and collective farms, and there has been evidence of income leveling for particularly successful lease teams. Leasing has also taken on a "campaign" atmosphere, with already existing collective contract teams being relabeled as lease teams (*arendnye podriady*, in comparison with true household leases) ("Polozhenie . . ." 1989). In this way state and collective farms can claim participation in the lease program without changing their operations in any essential way.

The state has done little to force the hand of farm management to restructure. In fact, recent financial policy has gone out of its way to make significant restructuring unnecessary. As part of the conversion to a "self-financing basis" which took place in 1988–89, subsidies to agriculture increased significantly (Table 2). In the Russian Republic in 1988, that republic's first year under "self-financing," the share of unprofitable state and collective farms declined from 19 percent to just 4 percent. Such a radical improvement was the result of higher prices paid rather than substantially reduced costs, as the increase in farm profits was accounted for by increases in farm subsidies. The improved performance apparently reflects a more effective means of coupling higher procurement prices with higher cost producers (Emel'ianov 1989; Kazakov 1988).

The developing imbalance in the economy as a whole has created strong justification for continued administrative presence in agriculture. The threat of runaway inflation has quelled calls for movement toward market allocation of resources, with the experience of Poland clearly understood. Without markets, attempts to improve and develop linkages throughout the system have been stifled. One example is in marketing. Changes in the way in which subsidies are channeled to farms have increased the incentive to sell to state procurement organizations rather than to develop cooperative or other marketing possibilities. (Previous input and other producer subsidies are now embedded in procurement prices for state sales. The new convertible ruble payments for above-quota sales of quality wheat, pulses, and oilseeds are also tied strictly to state sales.)

Even in areas where administrative intervention might serve to further agricultural restructuring, it is not occurring. For example, the state could be diverting more resources to the production of small-scale machinery and doing more to foster development of cooperatives throughout the agro-food sector. State-imposed barriers to entry are one of the major reasons why existing cooperatives have been able to charge high prices. Rather than pushing the further development of cooperatives, the state has been clamping down on their operation.

Recently, peasant associations have formed in a number of republics. It remains to be seen if they can function as effective advocates for the interests of lease holders and private farmers. Laws on land tenure and property rights are evolving at present. Three primary draft variants on land tenure law were submitted to the Supreme Soviet for consideration in the fall of 1989; one from the Council of Ministers, introduced by Ryzhkov at the Supreme Soviet session of October 2, one from the Lenin All-Union Academy of Agricultural Sciences (VASKhNIL) associated with VASKhNIL President A.A. Nikonov, and a more radical proposal submitted by VASKhNIL Academician V.A. Tikhonov.

Tikhonov's proposal calls for the outright denationalization of land and the possibility of private as well as collective ownership of land. Collective farm workers should have the option to take their share of the collective's capital and land and set up independent farms. For the 12,000 collective farms in serious financial trouble, it is not clear what assets farm workers will be able to claim (the per capita share may be quite small). Tikhonov's proposal does not specify, but also does not rule out, development of markets for land. Specific details are left to the determination of union republics and autonomous republics of the RSFSR (Liashenko 1989).

Under the other two proposals, land remains socialist property. Local soviets are in charge of monitoring and controlling land use. Markets for land under these proposals are not allowed. Both of them call for the introduction of land payments to replace differential prices as the means of rent extraction and as an incentive for more efficient land utilization. The Council of Ministers proposal is slightly more conservative, allowing for continued domination of state and collective farms in leasing arrangements, and the continued active role of the state in monitoring farm technology and land use (Liashenko 1989; "New Legislative Basis . . ." 1989).

During debate the Council of Ministers proposal came under attack for maintaining the role of state and collective farms as lessors when in fact they themselves are lessors in a sense. According to this point of view, local soviets should have sole right to lease land. While the Council of Ministers proposal leaves open the possibility of administrative oversight of farms' activity, debate of the proposals turned up strong support for legal guarantees for farms against such interference (Liashenko 1989).

Where to Go from Here?

Soviet efforts to revitalize agriculture to this point lack a system-wide coherence. Particular policies, such as changes in land tenure, even if radical and carried out in earnest, cannot by themselves solve the problem. A whole set of old taboos is blocking a comprehensive and successful restructuring. These include restrictions on: (1) private land tenure, and markets for land; (2) markets for inputs and output, i.e., agricultural activity outside of administrative control; (3) getting rich (the tendency to excessive income leveling); (4) "middleman" activities, the ability to earn income by overcoming imbalances associated with location and time; (5) disbanding a farm's operation (especially when this leaves rural inhabitants with no obvious employment options in the state economy). All of these restrictions can be associated either with the administrative nature of traditional Soviet agriculture or with equity considerations.

The 1990 plan does not imply significant changes in agricultural policy. The plan calls for increasing investment in the sector. Investment in the agro-industrial complex is slated to increase by about 10 percent, or roughly 6–7 billion rubles, while total investment in the economy may actually decline ("On the State Plan . . ." 1989). Budget subsidies to the agro-industrial complex will also increase in 1990 (Table 2). Much of the investment money in agriculture is to be spent for on-farm road construction and other "non-productive" uses, such as housing. The equity/efficiency trade-offs will continue to provide carrots to inefficient farms, while providing inadequate incentive to efficient producers. The goal of guaranteeing a sufficient profit level *(obespechit' uroven' rentabel'nosti)* remains prominent. This has traditionally been synonymous with adjusting final results rather than establishing a coherent and consistent system of rules within which farms operate.

Though the prospects for significant restructuring remain in real doubt, there have been some interesting innovations in Soviet financial and price policies in agriculture, either implemented or discussed, since 1988. In the last two years, subsidies for fertilizer and machinery were eliminated (farms were compensated by higher procurement prices). Fertilizer prices nearly doubled. This led Soviet farms to be more selective in their purchase of these inputs. Under the shift to "self-financing" introduced in 1988–89, a greater share of farm investment funds is being generated from own-revenue rather than credit or state budget allocation. (As noted above, this has been achieved by larger price subsidies.) Profitable farms are exhibiting greater care in the use of these funds. This was a point emphasized by farm managers with whom I met in the Moscow Oblast and the Ukraine in April 1988. The shift in investment funding and higher fertilizer and machinery prices led farms in the RSFSR to reduce their purchase of off-farm inputs and services by 8 percent in 1988, something probably unprecedented in the post-Stalin era (Kazakov 1989).

In early 1989 plans were announced for changes in Soviet procurement pricing policies in agriculture that included some interesting new aspects. The central feature is assimilation of quantity bonuses (and potentially the differential bonuses for weak farms also) into the base procurement prices, and significant aggregation of commodity pricing zones. The point is to relieve procurement prices of their function as an instrument for rental extraction. Instead, land payments would be introduced for this purpose (whether payments would be based strictly on land quality, or a broader set of criteria, is unclear). Subsidies for water use and crop insurance were also to be eliminated or reduced, with farms compensated through increases in procurement prices. Responsibility for most remaining direct producer subsidies, including costly investment in irrigation and drainage, has moved from the All-Union budget to Republican budgets, the hope being that Republican oversight will be more effective. One other important proposed change is the movement of price subsidies from the level of procurement, where most agricultural price subsidies are now paid, to the level of wholesale trade, thereby enhancing incentives to reduce losses in processing ("Po puti . . ." 1989).

The status of some of these proposals is now in doubt. There has been indication that the proposed changes in procurement prices and introduction of land payments have been postponed until 1991 or 1992.

Necessary changes in credit policy have not been initiated. With inflation estimated in the 8–10 percent range, interest rates remain fixed at 0.75–3 percent. Thinking on credit policy remains muddled. The head of the Agro-Industrial Bank has discussed the need for interest rate reform, but believes that rates should be differentiated based on a farm's ability to pay. That is, the "prime rate" should be reserved for the least reliable borrowers (Obozintsev 1988). In general, discussions of banking and credit reform betray a confused mix of a striving for greater efficiency and a commitment to equity-oriented social programs.

Thus far no farm has had to cease operations because of insolvency. In 1988, 37 state and collective farms in the RSFSR were declared bankrupt and are undergoing financial reorganization with the help of representatives of *Agroprombank*. One measure being used is to force farms to sell off inventories as a means of raising capital ("Authority . . . " 1989).

Conclusions

Why is restructuring of agriculture proceeding so slowly? Imbalances and stagnation in the economy underline the need for change, but also make this an unpropitious time for reform. Greater disbalances entail a greater adjustment under restructuring. The conventional wisdom in the USSR is that time is needed to redress current supply shortages before price reform is introduced. Of course, this is putting the cart before the horse; if supply shortages are eliminated there is no longer much need for a price reform. In the meantime the administrative-directive system, of necessity, remains intact with only minor changes. And the necessary underpinnning of a successful reform, a trusted and reliable currency, is becoming more and more an abstraction.

Agriculture is touted as a prime candidate to lead an economic restructuring, the belief being that sizeable production increases could be achieved with modest additional investment, if the proper incentives are put in place.[2] From the social point of view, restructuring of agriculture may have a very high price, however. Policies developed or magnified under Brezhnev, including guaranteed wages and lack of financial discipline generally, have created a situation where a significant number of Soviet farms, and the workers on those farms, are seriously threatened by a pro-efficiency reform. The state is not in a position to smooth the transition to a truly new system by expanding the pie. In comparison with China a decade ago, the USSR has fewer new carrots to offer. The state is pretty much unable to use additional subsidies or channel significantly more real resources into agriculture. (The quality of resources could be improved, but this entails time and reform of industry first.) The opportunity to work under heavily labor-intensive conditions, with inadequate up- and downstream support, is itself less of a carrot in the USSR than it is in China. Instead, carrots will have to be reallocated from inefficient to efficient producers.

Soviet policymakers have been reluctant to address the equity/efficiency trade-off. Equity considerations are particularly pertinent in agriculture, which is a repository for low-skilled workers and a place where, in comparison with industrial centers, alternative employment opportunities are limited. Before the administrative-directive system can be replaced in agriculture, a new set of "rules of the game" must be formulated (the most obvious option, markets with limited and clearly defined areas for government intervention) which are perceived as being legitimate. In the meantime, Soviet agricultural policies are attempting to do too much by trying to satisfy both equity and efficiency considerations simultaneously.

The very depth of the financial and economic problems in agriculture suggests that real restructuring is unavoidable over the longer term. Failure to restructure probably means continued sluggish growth in production (2 percent or less per year) and, barring retail price increases that are not compensated for by wage increases, a growing rather than declining burden on the state budget (through higher subsidies and/or debt write-off). There are already some optimistic signs in the areas of producer subsidies, land tax, procurement pricing, and land tenure. The hand of pro-efficiency points of view can be strengthened by positive experience in the Baltic Republics. The financial situation of agriculture there is better than for the country as a whole and more radical ideas about land tenure, pricing, and linkages appear close to implementation. For the USSR as a whole, the major hurdles on the path to restructuring remain uncleared, however, including consensus on new "rules of the game" and general realization that the cost of restructuring may be higher than originally anticipated.

A reform of agriculture in the USSR will need to open up alternative options for the rural economy, if potentially large social costs are to be minimized. In China, a burst in agricultural productivity associated with introduction of the household responsibility system and the freeing up of investment opportunities resulted in dynamic development of rural industry, services, and construction. Shortages of capital and uncertainties over allowed ownership forms need to be dealt with for anything like this to take place in the USSR. Successful diversification could both provide employment for excess labor in agriculture and improve the productivity of surviving farms.

Notes

1. Large producer price increases in China from 1978 to 1985 were financed by increases in retail price subsidies.
2. This could well be the case, though additional production would aggravate the storage, handling, and processing infrastructure, which is unarguably in need of significant new investment.

References

"Authority of the Credit Ruble" (1989). *Sel'skaia zhizn'* (April 15): 1–2. Translated in JPRS-UEA–89–022 (July 20, 1989): 52–55.

Cook, Edward C. (1988). "The Net Dependence of the Agro-Industrial Complex on the State Budget: A First Approximation." *CPE Agricultural Report* 1, no. 1: 17–19.

Emel'ianov, A. (1989). "Khozrashchet podlinnyi i mnimyi." *Ekonomicheskaia gazeta*, no. 19 (May): 7–8.

Kazakov, M.P. (1988). "Samofinansirovanie—v agropromyshlennyi kompleks." *Ekonomika sel'skokhozyaistvennykh i pererabativaiushchikh predpriiatii*, no. 2: 2–5.

——— (1989). "Samofinansirovanie: pervye itogi i perspektivy." *Ekonomika sel'skokhoziaistvennykh i pererabativaiushchikh predpriiatii*, no. 2: 2–7.

Liashenko, V. (1989). "Spor o zemle." *Sovetskaia Rossiia* (October 10): 1–2.

"New Legislative Basis for the Strategy of Deepening the Economic Reform. Report by N.I. Ryzhkov at the Second Session of the USSR Supreme Soviet" (1989). *Pravda* (October 3): 2–4. Translated in FBIS *Daily Report: Soviet Union* (October 4, 1989): 54–67.

Obozintseve, A.A. (1988). "Agroprombank i APK: vremia trebuet novykh form vzaimodeistviia." *Den'gi i kredit*, no. 3: 3–16.

"On the State Plan for the USSR's Economic and Social Development" (1989). *Pravda* (September 26): 2–4. Translated in FBIS *Daily Report: Soviet Union* (September 27, 1989): 49–64.

Petrov, V.V. (1989). "O zadachakh Agroprombanka SSSR v svete sovremennoi agrarnoi politiki." *Den'gi i kredit*, no. 7: 3–7.

"Polozhenie ob ekonomicheskikh i organizatsionnykh osnovakh arendnykh otnoshenii v SSSR" (1989). *Ekonomicheskaia gazeta*, no. 19: 7–8.

"Po puti novoy agrarnoi politiki" (1989). *Finansy SSSR*, no. 5: 1–7.

Puchkova, A.V. (1988). "Uluchshat' raspredelenie dokhodov v kolkhozakh." *Finansy SSSR*, no. 3: 46–51.

Semenov, V.N. (1989). "Sovershenstvovanie ekonomicheskikh otnoshenii v agropromyshlennom komplekse." *Ekonomika sel'skokhoziaistvennykh i pererabativaiushchikh predpriiatii*, no. 6: 2–6.

KAREN BROOKS

Lease Contracting in Soviet Agriculture in 1989

Lease contracting was endorsed in late 1988 and again in early 1989, but has not been widely adopted at the farm level. Concern about the poor response to this new alternative has led to new efforts to facilitate its adoption, and also to introduction of the individual proprietorship, a more radical departure from the contractual relations of traditional collectivized agriculture. Three pieces of legislation introduced in the last months of 1989 (the leasing law and draft laws on land and ownership) address potential leaseholders' and proprietors' reservations about the legal status of new forms of management. In mid-December, 1989, farms that contracted out all or a portion of their assets were offered the opportunity to write off debt in the same proportion.

Support for lease contracting at the highest levels of government and the party is divided, but no one speaks publicly against it. Rather, conservatives considered to be unenthusiastic about leasing argue that state and collective farms still have high potential as productive units, and that small-scale contracting should be purely voluntary, not implemented under pressure. As a purely voluntary program throughout 1989, leasing made little progress. The legislation and debt write-off at the end of the year were intended to make voluntary leasing more attractive. With marketing, pricing, and supply of inputs untouched by reform, however, leaseholders work under a sizeable handicap. The apparent inability to open marketing channels, reform prices, and deliver high quality agricultural implements suitable for small-scale production reduces incentives for agricultural workers and farm managers to take advantage of opportunities created by the new laws, both leasing and proprietorship. The hiatus in initiatives on pricing and marketing in agriculture threatens a serious loss of momentum in a sector vital for the success of the overall economic reform.

The author teaches in the Department of Agricultural and Applied Economics, the University of Minnesota.

Incentives and Contractual Choice
in Soviet Agriculture

Changes in remuneration and implicit contractual relations linking land and labor in Soviet agriculture have been central to efforts to increase productivity since the early 1960s, but they have had little success. The traditional work point system of the collective farm had, in theory, many characteristics of a team's payment regime. It was supplemented in the late 1960s and 1970s by straight wage contracts, and the team principle applied only to the bonus. In the early 1980s promotion of the collective contract was an attempt to revive the team as a unit of remuneration, but it was rejected by both managers and workers. In 1989 the lease contract, similar to an individual or team share tenancy, was introduced, but it, too, has failed so far to supplant the straight wage contracts. The individual proprietorship makes the proprietor residual claimant of net earnings, and is inconsistent with retention of straight wage contracts. The effort to change organization at the farm level throughout 1989 was thus a new stage in the attempt begun in the early 1980s to switch large numbers of workers off straight wage contracts to alternative forms of remuneration.

The effort raises two questions: (1) What is wrong with straight wage contracts in Soviet agriculture? and (2) Why, once in place, are they so difficult to supplant? A full answer draws on two separate but linked bodies of economic literature, the theory of incentives and organizational structure and that of contractual choice, but such completeness lies outside the limits of this paper.

Theoretical analysis of incentives in collectivized agriculture has usually employed two assumptions that limit its practical applicability to Soviet agriculture: the assumption that the team principle applies, and that an individual's contribution can be monitored without cost. Throughout the 1970s and 1980s Soviet agricultural workers have been on straight wage contracts with a high degree of job security and high costs of monitoring an individual's performance. Justin Yifu Lin has developed a model of a team with costly monitoring, in which the incentive to shirk is offset by the team's collective willingness to invest in an optimal degree of monitoring (Lin 1988). In the Soviet Union the dropping of the team principle and contemporaneous softening of the manager's budget constraint (through expansion of cheap credit and direct grants) removed the incentive for any monitoring of individual performance at all. Shirking increased, not only for labor, but for all inputs.

The literature on contractual choice helps explain why workers and managers separately would reject particular alternatives to the status quo, a contractual regime that offers relatively high returns with low risk, funded by the state budget and the banking system. Considerations of risk, return, interlinkage of factor markets, and imperfections in product markets define the set of alternatives that will be preferred to the current contractual regime (see, for example, Stiglitz 1974, and Bardhan 1989).

Lease Contracts *(arendnye kontrakty* or *podriady)*

Under the contracts an individual or small group agrees to manage assets belonging to a state or collective farm or individual proprietor in exchange for a rental payment. Lease contract groups are small, self-selected, and members are often related. The lessees do not receive a guaranteed wage, and instead earn residual profits according to the stipulations of the contract.[1] In the past, state or collective farms have been the lessors, but if the draft land law is passed, an individual proprietor could also lease out land.

There are two main forms of the lease contract as it is now being promoted. The first is called the targeted form. It is the more common and it binds producers quite closely to the parent farm. Targeted leases can be simply repackaged traditional labor contracts or genuinely new contractual relations, depending on the terms. A family, individual, or small group contracts to manage a portion of the farm's assets, including land, machinery, animals, and structures. All inputs and output are marketed through the parent farm. The contract specifies quantities of inputs that will be available and their prices, and sets a target quantity of output that should be delivered to the farm in fulfillment of the contract. The mechanism for collecting the rent is a difference between the price the lessee receives for output and the price at which the farm resells output to the state procurement organizations.

If the contracted minimal sale is enforced, this becomes a combination of fixed rent and share contract. The fixed rent is the difference between the contractual price and procurement price times the specified minimal delivery. Earnings on deliveries above the contracted minimum are shared, with the share determined by the ratio between the contractual and procurement prices. It is not likely that minimal deliveries can be enforced, and the targeted lease contract is best considered a share contract with threat of revocation in the following period if deliveries fall below the minimum. Another form of share contract is based on share of profit, not share of crop.

Targeted leases are intended now to be the main form of leasing. They allow the farm manager to specify the product mix and regulate the behavior of the lessee by threatening to withhold delivery of needed inputs. As long as farm managers are themselves still subject to state orders and sales quotas, they prefer targeted leases that allow them to retain control over the product mix and input distribution.

The second form of lease is the free contract, which is essentially a fixed rent contract. This is considered suitable for land and assets for which the manager of the parent farm has little alternative use. Small livestock operations in the Non-Black Soil Zone far from the central farm, or orchard, vegetable, and flower operations that are too labor-intensive for the parent farm to manage effectively are offered on fixed rent leases. Lessees under free leases market their own output, although they may market through the parent farm if both sides agree. They also can have their own accounts in the bank.

Data on adoption of lease contracting are scarce and unreliable. There appears to be no mechanism in place to monitor implementation or distinguish new contractual forms from old. Fragmentary data corroborate the anecdotal evidence that few people are signing leases. As of mid-1989 in the Russian republic, 43 percent of collective and state farms reported that they had signed at least one contract, and only 9 percent of agricultural workers were working under leases, some of which were undoubtedly not true leaseholds (Boev 1989, p. 8).

The observation that lease contracting is moving slowly has become generally accepted, and several reasons are often cited: (1) farm managers do not want to give up control over their assets; (2) potential lessees do not like to be completely dependent on the farm manager for supply of inputs and marketing of output; (3) potential lessees take on greater risk in exchange for expected returns that may not exceed the guaranteed wage; (4) even if they earn more, the increasing disequilibrium on consumer markets limits the value of their earnings; (5) the current pricing and marketing system discriminates against quasi-independent operators; and (6) leases do not provide security of tenure even if they are written for as long as fifty years.

This is a formidable list and seems quite adequate to explain the failure of the program so far. Yet there is another side to this failure. Financial discipline has not yet hardened the budget constraint that farm managers face. They are not yet forced by economic measures rather than political campaigns to make better use of their resources, particularly labor and land. Workers continue to draw secure and relatively high wages even though farms cannot afford to pay them out of their own productivity. Wages for employees of collective farms went up 8 percent in 1989 compared to 1988 (*Sel'skaia zhizn'*, October 29, 1989). This is slightly less than the average increase in non-agricultural wages (9 percent), but it exceeds increases in productivity. Many industrial enterprises funded excessive wage increases by using their new powers to raise prices, but most farms do not have those powers. When the farm cannot pay its bills, it applies for a special price premium or takes out another loan. The cost of fixed wage contracts with annual escalators shows up either in the state budget or in the accounts of the banking system.

The direct subsidy to pay the difference between costs to procure, process, and transport food and low retail prices in 1989 was 87.8 billion rubles, and is budgeted to grow in 1990 to 95.7 (*Ekonomicheskaia gazeta*, no. 40, October 1989, p. 11). The budgeted amount for 1990 represents a 30 percent increase since 1987. The large and growing food subsidy is a major food contributor to macroeconomic imbalance and the budget deficit, earlier reported as 120 billion rubles but recently revised to 92 billion (*Ekonomicheskaia gazeta*, no. 40, October 1989, p. 9). Three-quarters of the agricultural subsidy pays for meat and milk (Semenov 1987, p. 35).

The subsidy does not include farm indebtedness unless bad debts are written off the bank accounts and transferred to the budget. When the Food Program of 1982 went into effect in 1983, 9.7 billion rubles of bad debts were written off, and 11.1 billion rubles rescheduled for repayment to begin in 1991. Farm debt increased by ten billion rubles after the price increases of 1983, and additional debt was rescheduled in 1987. In 1987 collective and state farms held 34 percent of the total bank indebtedness, compared to 15 percent in 1970 (*Narodnoe khoziaistvo SSSR* 1987, p. 595). In 1988, 72 billion rubles constituting approximately half of total farm debt was rescheduled.

Gorbachev indicated in his speech to the March Plenum in 1989 that farm debt would not be written off because the budget could not absorb it. In December 1989, however, a massive (73.5 billion rubles) new debt write-off was announced. Farms experiencing fallout from Chernobyl and those being reorganized as agrarian subsidiaries of industrial enterprises will automatically be released from all debt. Other farms that offer a portion of their assets on lease can write off the same proportion of debt.[2] Much of the money loaned to farms has been used to cover payrolls, and its inflationary impact has already been absorbed. A wholesale write-off of farm debt without genuine restructuring of asset management at the farm level, however, would fuel a new cycle of inflationary indebtedness. It is not yet clear that targeted leasing, even if widely adopted, will provide the needed financial discipline and restructuring.

The financial problems of the agricultural sector at the farm level and the macro level are directly related to the failure of repeated attempts to reform the wage system. It is unlikely that farms will participate in the internal reorganization necessary to bring down costs of production and increase productivity as long as they can pass high costs on to the budget or the banking system. According to the latest published timetable for the reform, "toward the end of 1991, bankrupt collective and state farms will be reorganized as individual farms, cooperatives, etc." (*Ekonomicheskaia gazeta*, no. 43, 1989, p. 7). The new debt write-off calls this timetable into question, since bankrupt farms will be harder to recognize once shorn of their debt.

Terms of Contracts

The contractual process under current conditions inhibits the spread of lease contracting. Managers are under little pressure to sign contracts, and face no competition from neighboring farms in retaining their best workers. Productive workers have most to gain from leasing. The farm manager may, however, drive a much harder bargain with them than with shirkers whom he would like to get off the payroll, but who are reluctant to leave.

Productive workers cannot in practice negotiate with the manager of a neighboring farm unless they are willing to forfeit their homes and investment in household plots. Owner occupied housing and household plots are important assets for many rural families, and their disposition under leasing or individual proprietorship has not been clearly addressed. In the past, a family retained the right to occupy an owned home and farm a household plot only if a family member was a current or retired employee of the farm. If the family severed relations with the farm, the household plot was usually reassigned and the house sold or abandoned. Leaseholders or individual proprietors might want to quit their employment with the farm, but retain housing and the household plot. If they do not have the right to do so, some will opt for targeted intra-farm leaseholds simply to keep their housing.

As long as the lessee and lessor are expected to negotiate contracts in the absence of competitive markets, the process will be one of bilateral monopoly, with most of the power on the side of the farm manager. There are no systematic reported data yet on terms of leases, but reports from the agricultural press suggest that farms are exacting high rental fees from leaseholders. In an example reported from Tselinograd oblast, a leaseholding brigade sold wheat to the parent farm for seven rubles per centner, and the farm resold it to the procurement agency for thirteen (*Sel'skaia zhizn'*, 29 January 1988). It is unclear from the account who paid for seed, fuel, fertilizer, and other purchased inputs, but these are usually paid in full by the lessee. The leaseholder's share (54 percent) in this case seems quite low if it includes both labor and purchased inputs, but high if it is only labor. Another set of contractual prices reported from Orlovskaia oblast is also quite low (see Table 1).

These contract prices are very low, and suggest a share of at least 40 percent for the parent farm, although the full parameters of the contract are not reported. The share is probably even higher, since bonus payments raise farm prices above base procurement prices.

Concern about the level of rental payments has had two consequences. The leasing law and the draft law on land both assign the rural Council of People's Deputies the power to secure a land allotment (either leasehold or proprietorship) for any applicant qualified to work it. Workers dissatisfied with terms offered by their farm manager can apply to the Council of People's Deputies, but the extent to which the Council will be able to offset the manager's monopoly power has not yet been tested.

There is a growing demand for standard procedures for valuing contracted assets, particularly land. One set of guidelines issued in spring of 1988 by the All Union Scientific Research Institute for Agricultural Economics in Moscow calls for fixed rent payment for land or animals equal to planned or accounting profit *(pribyl')* for the asset in

Table 1. Contract Prices and State Procurement Prices (Vyshne-Ol'shanskii State Farm, Orlovskaia Oblast, 1988)

	Contract price	Procurement price
Grain	5.89 rubles per centner	10.50 (wheat)[a]
Sugar beets	2.75 rubles per centner	5.40[b]
Potatoes	8.28 rubles per centner	10-16[c]
Milk (winter)	28.00 rubles per centner	36.20[d]
Milk (summer)	18.00 rubles per centner	

[a]This is the average price for the RSFSR. The zonal price for Orlovskaia oblast may be lower, but not less than 9 rubles 70 kopecks. The price for this individual farm may differ from the zonal price. Rye is also grown in Orlov province. The state procurement price for rye on average in the RSFSR is 15 rubles per centner.

[b]Average for the RSFSR.

[c]Depending on quality and time of delivery.

[d]Average RSFSR, all seasons.

Sources: *Sel'skaia zhizn'*, August 2, 1988, and A. M. Chursin, *Tseny i kachestvo sel'skokhoziaistvennoi produktsii* (Moscow: Kolos, 1984).

the use specified by contract (*Rekomendatsii* 1988). This procedure requires a higher level of performance for the leaseholder than for the parent farm, since actual profit often falls short of planned profit. It also makes rental rates very sensitive to distortions in the price system and provides no linkage to land quality.

A subsequent set of guidelines issued in late 1989 by the same institute is seriously flawed (Boev 1989, p. 60). Negotiants are directed to take the net present value of the actual (not planned) average profit stream at an 8 percent discount rate to find a monetary value of a hectare of land. The monetary value is then augmented by the foregone earnings of the cash value of land over the duration of the lease (25 years) at the current rate of bank interest (0.5 percent annually). The resulting sum is to be divided by the duration of the lease to find an annual rental rate.

This odd procedure leads to the recommendation that short-term lessees pay more annually for the land than long-term leaseholders.[3] The double counting of net present value, first over an infinite horizon at 8 percent and then over a 25-year horizon at 0.5 percent, does relatively little harm because the bank rate is low. If it were more realistically related to the current inflation rate, the rental rate of land according to this methodology would far exceed what an agricultural producer might expect to earn from it under reasonable management.

The procedure is further flawed because it is based on profit, which includes return to factors other than land, as well as distortions in the price system. Workers on poorly managed farms would pay less for land of comparable quality than would those on better managed farms. This is perhaps consistent with the effort to switch the financially weak farms over to full-scale leasing, but a methodology based on marginal returns to land of comparable quality would be economically more justified. In most parts of the Soviet Union land quality has not been measured adequately to serve as a basis for setting user fees. The draft land law calls for a full land cadastre throughout the country to be carried out by the Council of Ministers of the USSR.

The leasing movement, sanctioned with enthusiasm in 1988 and endorsed again with fanfare at the March plenum on agriculture in 1989, appears now to have lost momentum. Expectations for voluntary leasing may have been too high initially, anyway. The Hungarian experience suggests that even when offered the opportunity to take out leases, many people on reasonably managed collective farms choose to retain the security of their farm employment, and enlarge their private plots or subsidiary holdings (Szelenyi 1988).

This hybrid blend of collective and private organization may not be viable in the long run, since costs of production on Hungarian collective farms remain high, and the ability of the state budget to absorb them is conditioned on the health of the macroeconomy. Yet it has apparent appeal to agricultural workers in an economic environment inhospitable to independent operators. The possibility of combining wage work and a leasehold or individual proprietorship has received little attention in Soviet discussions, but families may achieve it by allocating effort internally and regulating the size of the leasehold.

Few would argue that leasing should be mandatory or forced. Yet, if it is to remain voluntary and have a chance of success, the parameters within which voluntary decisions are made must be changed. An important change would be the imposition of fees for all users of agricultural land, not just leaseholders. Throughout 1989, leaseholders were expected to pay a rental fee to the parent farm for land that the farm received free of charge. The farm manager could collect returns to land either indirectly as producer rents or directly as rental payments from a leasehold. Underutilized land had an opportunity cost (foregone earnings from potential rental payments in excess of producer rents), but no direct cost. Furthermore, the opportunity costs may have been low if there was little known demand for leaseholds. If the farm manager and the lessee faced the same user fees for land, managers concerned about cash flow would actively seek lessees for underutilized land.

According to the draft land law, all users will pay for land, but the timetable for implementation of universal user fees is unclear. Fees will probably follow completion of the land cadastre, and in the meantime lessees and individual proprietors will be paying fees that state and collective farms do not.

The Legal Foundation
for Leasing and Proprietorship

Three pieces of new legislation bear directly on leasing and more generally on property relations in agriculture. The Basic Law of the USSR and Union Republics on Leasing was issued in draft form in September, formally passed on November 23, 1989, and took effect January 1, 1990 (*Ekonomicheskaia gazeta*, no. 49, December 1989, pp. 14–15). The draft version of the law on ownership was issued November 14, 1989 (*Ekonomicheskaia gazeta*, no. 48, November 1989, pp. 9–10). The draft version of the new land law was published on December 6 (*Izvestiia*, December 6, 1989). These pieces of legislation strengthen the legal foundation for property relations that deviate from those of traditional collectivized agriculture. They contain ambiguities and contradictions, however.

Many of the ambiguities relate to the status of land ownership. The ideological constraints on property relations involving land appear to be greater than those relating to other factors of production.

For example, the draft property law allows individual ownership of means of production except land. The law on leasing sanctions leaseholders' (but not proprietors') use of hired agricultural labor. Each of these is a significant departure from past ideological prohibitions. Yet, land remains in a special category. Each piece of legislation distinguishes between proprietorship of land *(vladenie)* and ownership *(sobstvennost')*. A proprietor cannot buy, sell, or mortgage the asset, while an owner has full rights of disposition, including sale and mortgage.

Individual proprietorship of agricultural land is sanctioned in each of the three pieces of legislation, and full private ownership with rights to purchase and sale is prohibited. (As a proposed exception, full private ownership of limited quantities of land for homes and dachas would be allowed; see Draft Land Law, addendum, article 5. This land could be bought and sold, but agricultural land could not.) Individual agricultural producers, small groups, or families would be granted life-time inheritable proprietorships or long-term leaseholds with user fees determined by the rural Council of People's Deputies. State and collective farms that stay in business would have rights of use but not proprietorship of their land and would pay user fees.

The legal assignment of land ownership promises to fuel rather than quiet controversy over the issue. There are four general categories of ownership of all property: by citizens, collectives, the state, and foreign entities. According to the draft law on ownership, land can be owned, and is included under state ownership. It is said, however, to belong not to the state but to "the people *(narod)* living on a given territory, to the Soviet people as a whole" (Part IV, article 23). The draft land law states that land is the property of "the people living on a given territory" with no mention either of the state or the Soviet people as a whole. Whether land is owned by the Soviet people, the people of the republics, or a lower territorial designation is unclear. An alternative version of the draft law on property proposed by the Supreme Soviet of Lithuania calls for land ownership by the republics (*Ekonomicheskaia gazeta*, no. 48, November 1989).

In comments on the draft land law, A. M. Emel'ianov, a member of the committee that drafted it, states that the committee rejected ownership of land by the national or republican governments in favor of ownership by the "people." Another commentator, People's Deputy and head of the subcommittee on new economic legislation, A. A.

Sobchak, states that according to the draft land law, land remains in state ownership, and land users pay rent to the owner (*Sel'skaia zhizn'*, October 26, 1989). Sobchak expressed the expectation that large numbers of proprietors or leaseholders could be on their land already in spring of 1990.

The law on leasing covers leasing in all sectors of the economy. The owner of resources has the right to lease them. State enterprises can lease physical assets that they control, but do not own. Land is in a special category, and can be leased in two ways. A potential leaseholder can seek an "intra-farm leasehold" by negotiating directly with the manager of the state or collective farm that holds the land and employs him or her. Alternatively, he or she can apply to the Council of People's Deputies, in which case the Council can seize an allotment of state or collective farm land and reassign it to the lessee. The Council then becomes the lessor of the land. Subleasing is permitted with restrictions (Part I, article 7).

The law states that the "corresponding" Council of People's Deputies (*sootvetstvuiushchie*) will have jurisdiction over division of land, but does not specify which council, whether village, district, or higher level. The land law is also vague in its reference to "corresponding" councils. In his commentary on the draft land law, Emel'ianov states that village councils are to apportion land (*Sel'skaia zhizn'*, October 28, 1989). The village councils were chosen in an effort to dilute the state and collective farm manager's monopoly power in questions of land disposition. Emel'ianov's commentary appears to be stronger than the language of the law, however. The draft law on ownership states that district and city, not rural, Councils of People's Deputies will distribute land for agricultural use, including leaseholds (Part IV, article 3).

The three pieces of legislation thus have conflicting language on who will distribute the land. They furthermore say little about how land will be distributed other than to note that laws at the level of the republic and autonomous region will govern procedures for confiscation of state and collective farm land for reassignment to individual proprietors and leaseholders. The rural Council of People's Deputies appears to have power, at least in the area of proprietorships, but there may be confusion regarding overlapping jurisdictions and appeal to higher territorial Councils. The ambiguity is greatest with regard to leasing, when the parent farm will retain use rights. It is unlikely that a lease could be imposed upon an unwilling state or collective farm if the lessee would be dependent on that same farm for purchased inputs, services, and marketing.

Despite their ambiguity, the laws alter the purely voluntaristic nature of leasing and proprietorship. Farm managers will no longer be able unilaterally to thwart the desire of workers to have access to land under new contractual relations. Implementation of the laws and testing of new property relations promises to be contentious.

The leasing law clearly states that the output of leased property belongs to the lessee (Part I, article 9). Leaseholders have expressed concerns that without ownership of their assets they could not defend ownership of the product, and the courts have on at least one reported instance confirmed their fears. A state farm repossessed fattened cattle from a leaseholder without contracted compensation, and the court found in the farm's favor (*Sel'skaia zhizn'*, October 14, 1989). The two issues in the case concerned the leaseholder's right to ownership of a non-land asset (the cattle) and to the product of leased assets (weight gain). The law on leasing states that the leaseholder owns the product outright, and can purchase leased assets (except land) through negotiation with the farm manager.

The draft land law, however, states that the proprietor *(zemlevladel'ets)* of land has ownership *(sobstvennost')* of crops and structures on his or her land. The proprietor may lease out land, but according to a strict reading of the draft land law, it appears that the proprietor retains ownership of crops even on leased land. The law on ownership states that the leaseholder has full ownership of the produce of leased assets, and that all leased assets except land may be individually purchased by the leaseholder.

The three pieces of legislation together provide a legal framework for expansion of small holding, both through leasing and independent proprietorship. The mechanism for redistributing land is not clear and the methodology for valuation has not yet been chosen. Prohibitions on the purchase and sale of land will be costly if retained in the long run, but may be useful now. Disequilibrium in the asset market would rapidly drive land prices up if land could be bought and sold now, and would defeat the effort to allow a class of "proprietor-operators" to emerge.

In July 1989, Lithuania passed a law legalizing private proprietorship of up to 50 hectares of land if it is used as a family farm (*Pravda*

Litvy, July 9, 1989). The land cannot be sold or mortgaged and cannot be rented, although the term for rent *(vnaem)* is different from the term used for lease *(arenda)*. Farmers who want to start a family farm with land owned by their family prior to collectivization (or other land) apply to the executive committee of the local council of people's deputies. A local commission set up by the Council of Ministers of Lithuania takes the application, surveys and values the land, and oversees the transfer.

Lease Contracts and the Collective Contract

The precursor to the lease contract was the collective contract. As late as the fall of 1987, the collective contract brigade was hailed in the Soviet agricultural press as the most progressive form of organization of agricultural labor. Yet, by mid-1988, the collective contract had been eclipsed by its successor, the lease *(arendnyi)* contract, and exposed as a transitional, ineffective, and unpopular form.

Collective contracts began to appear in significant numbers in the early 1980s, and the campaign was increasingly associated with Gorbachev personally.[4] In his address to the Party Plenum in July 1988, Gorbachev noted that since 1983 he had made a major effort to promote the collective contract in various forms. Under the collective contract, a group of workers negotiated with the farm management to perform a set of tasks in exchange for a specified payment. The group monitored the performance of its members and divided earnings accordingly.

The contracts included elaborate restatements of labor norms and bonus payments for specific tasks. Brigades were encouraged to implement monitoring and accounting schemes using the "coefficient of labor participation [KTU]" to apportion the new bonus among themselves. This was essentially the work point system of the pre-Brezhnev era, and workers who violated discipline could be docked points in the final division of earnings. The collective contract as originally conceived was consistent with the effort to instill tighter labor discipline. Since the pay of each brigade member depended at least in part on the performance of the team, tolerance for widespread shirking and lax discipline was expected to diminish.

Alchian and Demsetz argue in their classic article on the nature of the firm that monitoring labor performance is costly, and that a monitor has an incentive to do the job only if he or she is a residual claimant to earnings net of payments to other inputs (Alchian and Demsetz 1972). The collective contract system shifted the monitoring function to brigade members and made them residual claimants of income. It also imposed upon them a form of organization that had high costs of monitoring and accounting. Use of the new work point system was cumbersome and tied brigade members to the old norms for job performance. Many of the original brigades were large; the average in reported data is twenty-five, but many were larger still. Membership was diverse and not self-selected. The work point system with a heterogeneous work force was cumbersome and costly to administer. Few brigades bothered to use the work point system, and distributed bonuses in proportion to base pay, as they had under the old system. By 1987 the use of the work point system was rarely praised or even mentioned.

The collective contract brought higher, not lower costs of production. The director of a state farm in Orlovskaia oblast reported that the farm's yields increased significantly with adoption of the collective contract, but so did costs of production: "Contract collectives tried to increase output at any price, and did not take costs into account" (Sel'skaia zhizn', August 2, 1988). Costs rose in part because workers negotiated wage increases as a price for monitoring themselves. The base tariff wage became the advance payment for workers on collective contract brigades, and payment according to output functioned much as the bonus under the old system. Higher wages coupled with poor control over purchased inputs pushed costs of production up. The collective contract thus not only failed to ameliorate the existing financial crisis in agriculture, but worsened it.

The collective contract brigade was an unstable organization. Between 1985 and 1987 there were many reports of brigades dissolving and reconstituting themselves in what amounted to a search for lower monitoring costs. Brigades reported as successful in the press were increasingly small brigades, although the official aggregate data do not show much diminution. This is probably because the aggregate data include the wholesale rechristening of large traditional brigades as collective contract brigades, and the simultaneous breakup of older collective contract brigades into smaller self-selected and family units.

The weak agricultural program prior to 1988 put additional and unrealistic expectations on gains to be realized from the collective contract. When asked at the 1987 Joint Soviet Economy Roundtable "Why not take agriculture first, instead of starting with industry—the hardest sector of all?'' Abel Aganbegyan responded, ''We did start first with agriculture by establishing Gosagroprom and encouraging introduction of the collective contract'' (Aganbegyan 1987).

Despite glasnost, mounting evidence that the collective contract was not working surfaced only when the deteriorating financial crisis in agriculture in late 1987 forced a re-evaluation of agricultural policy (Brooks 1988). Profiles of successful *arendatory* replaced those of the collective contract brigades, and many brigades reconstituted themselves under new lease contracts.

The proportion of the work force working under collective contracts continued to increase as individuals and farms still on the wage system switched over to collective contracts. Even while the numbers went up, however, disenchantment with the collective contract and its results was openly expressed. At the March Plenum (1989), Gorbachev reaffirmed his commitment to the collective contract, but observed, ''Experience has shown that there are more radical forms of management now based on long term leasing of land and other means of production with full financial independence'' (*Sel'skaia zhizn'*, July 30, 1988, p. 2). He went on to advocate lease contracts of twenty-five or even fifty years duration.

Gorbachev and other leaders stress the financial autonomy and responsibility of the tenant, and by implication underscore the failure of the collective contract to bring the desired cost savings. Prime Minister Ryzhkov commented on the Law on Cooperatives in May of 1988, ''After all, the state is not responsible for the activities of any form of cooperative'' (*Ekonomicheskaia gazeta*, no. 21, May 1988, p. 10). The same is true for a leaseholder working under contract.

Lin's model of a team with costly monitoring of individual effort can be used to explain the failure of the collective contract (Lin 1988). The team principle was used only for a portion of earnings amounting usually to about 20 percent; collective contract remuneration was linked closely to the wage tariff. It did not pay for workers to assume monitoring costs for such a small portion of pay, and the continued soft budget constraint provided little incentive to impose monitoring.

Straight Wage Contracts
Prove Resilient if Inefficient

Khrushchev monetized agricultural earnings by raising wages on state farms and increasing the value of the work point on collective farms.

In 1966 Brezhnev directed collective farms to abandon the work point system and begin paying workers according to the wage scale of state farms (Johnson and Brooks 1983; Wädekin 1989). With this, the entire agricultural work force became hired laborers on straight wage contracts with a high degree of job security.

The wage contracts and soft budget constraints at the farm level contributed to escalating costs of production during the 1970s, growing farm debt, and an increasing burden of direct subsidy to the sector. Workers and farm managers rejected the collective contract by adopting it fully and transforming its substance to the old straight wage contract with higher wage levels. Lease contracting may suffer the same fate unless financial discipline is imposed and wages are limited to what the farms can afford to pay under a rational pricing system. The new debt write-off program says remarkably little about financial discipline. Changes in marketing, credit, input supply, and access of rural people to consumer goods are needed before opportunities to work more efficiently and independently will appeal to many workers.

The likelihood that this kind of sweeping change can be designed and implemented from the center now appears low. The current emphasis on regional autonomy suggests that republics will be encouraged to draft their own agricultural policies. This presents an unprecedented opportunity for republics such as the Baltics to try their own agricultural reforms. It also presents the danger that each region will strive for regional self-sufficiency with resulting reduction of comparative advantage and gains from interregional domestic trade.

Notes

1. Workers on genuine lease contracts would not receive guaranteed wages, but many targeted lease contracts may be written with implicit guaranteed wages. Targeted leases appear to be rather easily subverted into straight wage contracts, and heavy reliance on targeted leasing may replicate the fiasco with the collective contract. Furthermore, both targeted and free leases usually contain clauses releasing the lessee from contractual obligations if events "outside his control" reduce yields. These clauses could easily be interpreted to support guaranteed wages as minimal remuneration for workers.

2. This could be an invitation for widespread adoption of fictitious leases. Unless the debt write-off is coupled with financial discipline, it will lead to another build-up of debt to cover current expenses.

3. Perhaps it is feared that leaseholders will mine the fertility of the soil, and therefore short-term lessees should pay more than long term leaseholders, if the long-term leases are binding on both parties. This line of reasoning, however, is

not behind the recommended rates. Furthermore, if deterioration in soil quality is feared, it should be addressed by policy instruments other than differentiated rental rates.

4. Analysis of the collective contract in agriculture and the optimistic assessment in 1987 of its potential by Soviet commentators and some foreign observers can be seen in V. P. Gagnon, Jr., "Gorbachev and the Collective Contract Brigade," *Soviet Studies* 39 (January 1987): 1–23.

References

Aganbegyan, A.G. (1987). "Basic Directions of *Perestroika.*" *Soviet Economy* 3, 4 (October–December): 277–97.

Alchian, A.A., and H. Demsetz (1972). "Production, Information Costs, and Economic Organization." *American Economic Review* 62 (December).

Bardhan, Pranab (1989). *The Economic Theory of Agrarian Institutions.* New York: Oxford University Press.

Boev, Vasilii R. (1989). *Razvitie arendnykh i podriadnykh otnoshenii v agropromyshlennom komplekse (rekomendatsii).* Moscow: VNIESKh.

Brooks, Karen M. (1988). "The Law on Cooperatives, Retail Food Prices, and the Farm Financial Crisis in the USSR." Staff Paper, Department of Agricultural and Applied Economics, No. P88–29 (September).

Gagnon, V.P., Jr. (1987). "Gorbachev and the Collective Contract Brigade." *Soviet Studies* 39 (January): 1–23.

Johnson, D. Gale, and Karen M. Brooks (1983). *Prospects for Soviet Agriculture in the 1980s.* Bloomington: Indiana University Press.

Lin, Justin Yifu (1988). "The Household Responsibility System in China's Agricultural Reform: A Theoretical and Empirical System." *Economic Development and Cultural Change* 36, no. 3 (April): S199-S224.

Rekomendatsii po organizatsii arendnogo podriada v sel'skokhoziaistvennom proizvodstve Moskovskoi oblasti. VNIIESKh VASKhNIL (1988).

Semenov, V. (1985). *Prodovol'stvennaia programma i finansy.* Moscow: Finansy i statistika.

——— (1987). "Sovershenstvovanie finansogo mekhanizma agropromyshlennogo kompleksa." *Ekonomika sel'skogo khoziaistva,* no. 9: 31–39.

Stiglitz, Joseph E. (1974). "Incentives and Risk Sharing in Sharecropping." *Review of Economic Studies* 41 (April): 219–56.

Szelenyi, Ivan (1988). *Socialist Entrepreneurs: Embourgeoisement in Rural Hungary.* Madison: University of Wisconsin Press.

Wädekin, Karl-Eugen (1989). "The Re-Emergence of the Kolkhoz Principle." *Soviet Studies* 41, no. 1 (January): 20–38.

DON VAN ATTA

"Full-Scale, Like Collectivization, but without Collectivization's Excesses"
The Campaign to Introduce the Family and Lease Contract in Soviet Agriculture

Since the Twenty-seventh Congress of the Communist Party met in early 1986, Soviet agricultural policy has been transformed.[1] The changes are still being debated, and they will not all be implemented soon. But the regime has committed itself to allowing various forms of agricultural organization to co-exist in the countryside for the first time since Stalin's mass collectivization imposed the standard model collective farm and destroyed individual peasant farming throughout the country in the early 1930s.[2] Families, individuals, and small cooperatives are now being encouraged to lease land, equipment, and buildings from the existing farms or local soviets. General Secretary Gorbachev intends to create an agrarian sector in which state, collective, cooperative, and individual peasant farms, as well as the private plots of kolkhozniki and sovkhozniki, coexist with equal legal rights and jointly solve the country's food problems ("Ob agrarnoi . . ." 1989; USSR Council of Ministers 1989).

As in every other effort to alter rural society since full-scale collectivization itself, the party-state authorities have launched a campaign of administrative pressure to implement their desired changes. This essay examines that drive. After a brief description of the general purposes and characteristics of administrative campaigns in the Soviet Union, the particular innovations to be introduced are outlined, the history of the movement is summarized, and the politics shaping it are suggested. Finally, the chances for success and implications of the intertwined movements to restore family-based farming and introduce the lease contract in agriculture are considered.

Unlike previous drives to change the organization and payment of

---

The author teaches in the Department of Government, Hamilton College.

work on the farms, the drive to introduce the family-based lease campaign openly challenges the standard structure and management of the kolkhozy and sovkhozy.[3] It is also an integral part of Gorbachev's perestroika, a general effort to reshape the Soviet political system. The general secretary's ideas on agricultural reform have evolved along with the rest of his strategy, and the history of the campaign is closely connected to other struggles about the future of the Soviet system. Because it challenges the kolkhoz-sovkhoz structure, the family-lease campaign is both more likely to succeed than other movements for organizational change in agriculture conducted since the 1930s and more dangerous to the existing distribution of political power in the countryside.

Administrative Campaigns

Since the 1930s, the Soviet party-state has both orchestrated campaigns and directed mobilizations by the party and state authorities to get agricultural work done. Although the means are no longer quite as crude as those used in the first years of the system, demands for reports of successful completion of interim tasks, the issuing of orders directly from the party district committee (raikom) over the heads of farm managers, and the sending of local party workers out to the farms continues to be standard practice, even in the Gorbachev era. Innovations in farm organization or agricultural practice are still normally introduced by campaign as well.

Innovation campaigns differ from routine "management" campaigns in their purpose, but not their methods. An organizational change successfully applied to one or a few farms catches higher authorities' attention. It is then approved by these authorities in a resolution, speech, or Pravda editorial "recommending" the innovation. Once the signal is given, the nationwide campaign machinery begins to operate. Exemplary farms or their subunits where the change has brought outstanding results are widely publicized. The models are inundated by visitors from other farms who come "for the experience," and the model workers find much of their time taken up by explaining what they have done. Other areas begin to report successful introduction of the novelty. Local and regional authorities naturally desire to show how quickly and well they can introduce the new method, and their wish to excel in their superiors' eyes is often reinforced by plan targets for introduction of the new method. Within a relatively short time, two or three years at the most, farm managers and *raikom* secretaries report the entire country's farms have adopted the change.

Although these innovation campaigns have always reported success, and they have often succeeded in such formal tasks as redrawing farm boundaries, most of them have actually failed either to gain general adoption or to affect productivity. Attempts to reorganize farm work, such as the drive for rural Stakhanovites in the 1930s, the establishment of complex links in the 1960s, or the general introduction of the Ipatov method in the 1970s have done little or nothing to solve the problems which they were intended to address. Within a few years, post-mortems in the Soviet press have found that they affected little except the reports and the farmers' nerves.[4] Such failed drives, and the "command-administrative" management style they epitomize, are derisively referred to in the Soviet press as "campaign-ism."

In the absence of economic incentives or political instruments able to check the actions of the party-state administrative hierarchy, however, the Soviet state has had no alternative to campaigns as a tool for introducing change. Yet the regime's very lack of alternative implementation mechanisms is one key reason why campaigns for organizational change generally fail either to be widely adopted in reality (as opposed to on paper) or to have much economic impact.

The political elite generally has not been united around the necessity or desirability of change. Personal and factional rivalries, or genuine policy differences, may cause leaders to oppose ideas just because their opponents propose them. The party and ministerial apparat, the officials charged with making the system function and implementing policies, may not understand the innovation, oppose it because their patrons in the elite do so, or fail to implement it because it goes against either their perceived interests or the immediate needs of "getting the work done." Understanding that innovation campaigns tend to come and go, local officials, farm managers, and rank-and-file farmers often choose to ignore the whole business and hope it will go away or at least drag their feet on changing more than the names of work groups and the categories and numbers on the endless reports they send their superiors.

The mid-1960s decisions to increase agricultural investment created a powerful constituency opposed to reform. Most of the new money devoted to rural areas went to salary increases, more capital equipment, and construction of expensive livestock facilities and reclamation works. This reinforced the power of regional party officials who could use the cash to buy political support. Much of it was eventually funneled to heavy industrial (machine-building and construction) interests that have traditionally dominated decisions about resource allocation in the Soviet Union.

Campaigns to change the organization of farm workers are especially prone to fail because they generally seek to make the peasants take more initiative in planning and carrying out agricultural operations. But the kolkhoz system was designed to stifle peasant initiative, and continues to do so. The rational peasant is seldom willing to take risks. The farm authorities have many ways to enforce their will on him, while he has few levers for affecting them. The peasants on Adylov's sovkhoz in Uzbekistan, who were imprisoned in the director's private jail, were assigned to building endless, useless rock walls as penal labor, and "disappeared" if they complained, may have been in a particularly bad situation; their extreme situation demonstrates the potential power of all kolkhoz managers and sovkhoz directors over their farmers (Sokolov 1988).

An innovation campaign, like any drive to implement reform in the Soviet context, then, can only succeed when the elite is united on its necessity, the party-state apparatus can somehow be coerced into implementing it, and managers and rank-and-file farmers can be convinced that the innovation is not too risky for them to work in the new way.

Unlike previous campaigns, the current one attempts to change the whole kolkhoz system and state administrative structure. To the extent that it changes the system, its chances for success are greater than those of previous campaigns, in part because it may create organized interest groups, such as peasant associations, with a stake in completing and defending the changes. Because the family farming and lease campaign differs from previous campaigns by openly challenging the existing organizations and power relations in the countryside, its success may be as dangerous for the regime as its failure. The current drive may fail because it is only formally implemented and really changes nothing. But the regime might also lose control of the campaign as the internal logic of the reforms it promotes drives some local officials and farmers to demand its extension, perhaps to complete decollectivization, which would challenge the bases of the party's claim to authority and its political power. The danger that a mobilization directed from above might escape the control of those leaders who inspired it is inherent in any campaign, but this campaign is potentially more threatening than most because it seeks to change the regime's structure without toppling it.

Family and Small-Group
Contracts—Peasant Farming

Since collectivization, Soviet farmers have normally worked in large groups, called brigades, performing individually assigned and evaluated tasks assigned to them by the brigade leader on a daily, or almost-daily, basis. Workers are paid according to their fulfillment of these short-term assignments, and little attention is devoted to the end result, the harvest. This system was borrowed from industry because of its supposedly greater efficiency. It also reduced the influence of the peasant household by stripping it of economic functions.

Family crews began to be openly used and celebrated in labor-short areas, particularly the Orenburg oblast' in Siberia, in the early 1970s. By 1979, a socialist competition of family crews had been nationally publicized (Shabanov 1976; "Orenburgskie . . ." 1979). "Family teams" were occasionally reported in the early 1980s as well. However, the idea of a "family contract," in which a group of blood relations received its own plot of land and equipment for several years, emerged only after Gorbachev came to power.

Agricultural economist V.Ia. Uzun defines the innovation:

> Small-group or family forms [of labor and production organization] include primary subunits of a communal farm—a sovkhoz, kolkhoz, interfarm enterprise—on which production is carried out by the members of one or several families which have agreed among themselves. Such a subunit consists more often than not of two to five able-bodied workers. It is given land—an integrated [*osvoennym*] or specially-demarcated crop rotation—cattle and other productive resources for a lengthy period (10–15 years) (Uzun 1987, p. 5).

In plain language, this is a (peasant) family farm, since with such "family contracts," as agricultural economist Gelii Shmelev (1986) wrote, "the family becomes the basic independent production cell of a farm." Restoring the family unit to the center of Soviet agriculture in many ways undoes collectivization, whether or not the collective and state farms are formally disbanded. Doing so, of course, raises critical questions about the legitimacy of the Soviet state and Communist party rule, as well as acute practical questions about just how the strengths of the family unit can once again be employed in the countryside. Use of the lease contract *(arendnyi podriad)* by families and other small groups offers a way to do so.

The Lease

As is usually the case with Soviet innovations, it can be difficult to determine just exactly what the innovation to be implemented really is. One reason for this is a natural tendency by the apparatus and the farmers to fuzz over just what they are doing in order to make their reports look better while also allowing them to disavow what might turn out to be a failed campaign. Another reason is the dynamic of the campaign itself. Regulations, laws, and directives defining the *arenda* have emerged over three years, and they do not always coincide perfectly. Oblast' and republican level recommendations, presumably based on local experiments, were published first, often in small-quantity departmental prints. On August 25, 1988, the USSR Gosagroprom approved recommendations on the lease contract for the entire country. The recommendations included a form for the contract agreement, requiring only that the blanks be filled in.[5] In February 1989, a model statute *(polozhenie)* appeared. This document specified all the manifold accounting details and documents needed to organize lease groups ("Polozhenie . . ." 1989). General legislation came out still later, with an April 7, 1989, Supreme Soviet Presidium *ukaz* and finally the law on the *arenda* (lease) in December 1989.[6] As this is written, basic questions about land ownership remain undecided. However, economist Pavel Bunich is probably correct when he says that the lease system is a way to put the concept of various forms of property into practice which will work with whatever forms of property the Soviet legislature finally decides to establish (Nikitin 1989).

Soviet law now provides two different kinds of lease. Any individual citizen, registered group of citizens (a cooperative), or state enterprise may lease land and productive assets from any state or cooperative enterprise willing to do so. For instance, a ministry may lease part of a plant to a cooperative, often made up of the plant's employees and managed by the former state-employed manager. In agriculture, individuals or cooperatives may apply to the local Soviet for a lease on any vacant land. However, most agricultural land is already worked by state farms, collective farms, or industrial enterprises' subsidiary farms, which hold agricultural land with the right of permanent use *(postoiannoe pol'zovanie)*. These farms may lease land to individuals and groups, whether or not they have been kolkhoz members or farm employees, on an intrafarm lease *(vnutrikhoziaistvennaia arenda)*, also called a lease sub-contract *(arendnyi podriad)*. As the Russian prefix *pod-* (under) indicates, this is not a contract between equals, but an agreement reached between a dominant and a subordinate party.

The *arendnyi podriad* is primarily a labor agreement. The USSR Law on the Arenda embodies this distinction between the lease and the lease contract. A lessee *(arendator)* on a lease is a legal person and can do business with parties of his own choosing. A lessee on *arendnyi podriad* is not a juridical person and can normally dispose of his produce, at least up to a planned and agreed amount, only to the lessor *(arendodatel')*. The lessor may, but is under no obligation to, allow the lessee to open his own bank account and sell his produce to outside parties. Disputes arising under an *arenda* are to be settled by the state arbitration service *(gosarbitrazh)* or an appropriate court, while disputes about an *arendnyi podriad* are to be settled in accordance with USSR and Union-Republican labor law.[7]

The agricultural *arendnyi podriad* developed from a tradition of subcontracting farm work for a relatively lengthy period to a particular group of farmers. That tradition has always been contentious because it is counterposed to the system of daily work-orders *(nariady)* and piece-rate pay for short-term work traditional on Soviet farms. Experiments with such contracts have sometimes been condemned because the political authorities thought they masked the breakup of the kolkhozy.

The first written subcontract in Soviet agriculture was the *akkord*. This agreement, whose name was deliberately borrowed from a foreign language in order to emphasize that it was not a "contract" *(dogovor)*, was the heart of Khrushchev's sovkhoz wage reform in the early 1960s. Large groups of workers would contract with the farm to carry out an entire task, not just the day's job. The *akkord* group might even take on a whole crop. The agreement set limits on anticipated expenditure of seeds, fertilizer, fuel, and other current costs, as well as specifying the price per unit of output to be paid the farmers. However, these quasi-contracts had little practical effect. The brigades concluding them were very large, often sixty to a hundred workers. They did not exist, in fact or law, outside of the farm which gave them the "contract," and so the brigades' members had no way to enforce the accord when the farm or higher authorities violated or unilaterally changed it. Contract terms were based on the farm's planned prices and wages were set by summing the potential piece-rate earnings for each job involved in growing the particular crop. When farmers doubled or tripled yields, farms frequently failed to pay them as the accord provided because fulfilling the agreement would exceed the farm's wages budget. So, the accord became just another document prepared by the brigadier for each year's work, usually without the consent and sometimes without the knowledge of his workers.

The accord developed into the "accord and premium" system of agricultural pay legalized for all kolkhozy as well as sovkhozy in the 1969 revision of the kolkhoz model charter. With this system, farmers were paid a bonus for exceeding planned output specified in the accord.

Because output could not be known until the end of the season, the accord system provided for advancing the farmers' money against their anticipated earnings. When the advances were based on piece-rate pay, the accord often became a dead letter, since farmers worked to maximize their advance rather than their long-term earnings (especially when, as was very frequently the case, the plan on which the accord was based could not be fulfilled in any case). However, kolkhozy could get permission to pay advances based on time-rates as an experiment in the late 1960s, and the 1969 model charter provided that all kolkhozy could pay advances based simply on the number of hours or days worked rather than piece-rate output. Pay based on an accord and premium with time-rate advances *(akkordno-premial'naia sistema s povremennym avansirovaniem)* dispensed with timekeepers and daily accounting, as well as the daily work orders, and so came to be called "work-order-less" *(beznariadnaia),* or "autonomous," wages.

Never formally condemned, the *beznariadnaia* system fell out of favor in the early 1970s. Most farms continued to pay their workers based on daily piece-rates. When the same system reappeared in the early 1980s, it was called the collective, or brigade, contract *(brigadnyi podriad),* but this was only a new name. The official recommendations for the two systems are substantially identical. Like the original accord system, the brigade contract was only concerned with current production expenses and wages. Farm workers were not required to pay for equipment, land, or buildings.

Not surprisingly, the press has repeatedly complained that farmers operating on the autonomous or brigade contract system pay little attention to input costs, preserving the land, or maintaining equipment, instead seeking to maximize their immediate production. Some of these complaints have been excuses for reasserting the traditional close control over farm workers. But it is also eminently logical that a farmer, told to maximize his income, aware that after he does it the plan will likely be raised, and with no particular reason to care for the future of the land or equipment, should behave in this short-sighted way.

Unlike the brigade contract, the agricultural lease contract forces farmers to pay for their capital equipment and land. Farmers will now have an incentive to care for the land and their equipment. Since farmers will not want to pay for unnecessary capital goods, this change will also, it is hoped, brake the farms' tendency (typical of all sectors in a mature Soviet-style economy) to constantly demand more and more investment. Land ownership always remains with the state. Land rental is either at a fixed annual rate or a percentage of annual profits. Once capital goods and buildings have been fully amortized by the rental payments, their ownership can pass to the *arendator.*[8]

By replacing the system of guaranteed piece-rates with earnings based on final production, the lease solves the problem of individual incentives inherent in the daily piece-rate system, which gave individuals little reason to work well or carefully. The statute on the *arendnyi podriad* provides that on farms which have entirely transferred to the lease system, piece-rate accounting is no longer done. The lessee agrees to take whatever remains of his income from sale of produce after his costs are paid. However, since the prices for his produce are determined either by state procurement prices or intrafarm *(raschetnye)* prices, his income still ultimately depends on the central plan.

The law on the *arenda* guarantees long-term (fifty-year) leases. It presumes that leases will normally be renewed, and allows the lease to be inherited by a family member who has been working on the property. Although under current legislation, the farmers do not own the land nor can they sell the right to use it, these tenure provisions allow family farming for the first time since collectivization.

History of the Campaign

The campaign for the implementation of the *arendnyi podriad* and a variety of farm organizations grew out of the failure of a preceding drive to introduce the brigade contract. As already noted, the brigade contract paid groups of workers, rather than individuals, depending on the final results of their work—the harvest. The brigade contract campaign began before Brezhnev's death in 1982 and unfolded with full force during Yuri Andropov's short period of leadership. Politburo approval of that innovation was signaled at a Central Committee–sponsored conference held on a Belgorod oblast kolkhoz in 1983 which was addressed by then CPSU Central Committee secretary for agriculture Mikhail Gorbachev.[9]

During his first year as general secretary, Gorbachev showed little public inclination to radically change Soviet agriculture. Instead, he repeatedly demanded that existing mechanisms be made to work better, pushing palliatives like the brigade contract. The creation in November of that year of the USSR Gosagroprom, a "super-ministry" combining a number of ministries concerned with agriculture and food processing into one agglomeration, exemplifies this tendency to streamline an existing system, rather than to change it.

The Political Report of the Central Committee Gorbachev delivered at the Twenty-seventh Party Congress in early 1986 did not suggest much bigger changes to come. The general secretary asserted that economic methods of administering agriculture were to be emphasized, expanding the independence, while increasing the responsibility of the farms for their results—a contradictory promise made by all his post-Stalin predecessors. Losses, running as high as 30 percent of some crops, would be reduced. The policy of substantial capital investment in equipment, buildings, and infrastructure would be continued, and constant concern for the living conditions of farmers would be shown. Although the report revived Lenin's NEP slogan of the "tax-in-kind" *(prodnalog),* implicitly promising a reform of the procurement system and its marketization, it also favorably mentioned the creation of new, centralized administrative units such as Gosagroprom. Better plan normatives would be developed, and plans would be stable over the whole five-year plan period (another promise lifted from the past and always previously violated). Gorbachev also promised to continue the brigade contract campaign, mentioning "brigades, teams and families" as appropriate units to contract for "means of production, including the land" ("Politicheskii . . ." 1986, pp. 52–53). These phrases hinted at change, but only very slightly. The mention of families as work units rejected the Stalinist ideological assumption that peasant households should not be allowed to serve as both social and economic units lest they take on a political (and oppositional) cast as well. Contract brigades had always been assigned land for the duration of their contracts, however, so that ambiguous reference might or might not foreshadow a change in past practice.

The joint party and state resolution on agricultural reform which followed the Congress made no radical changes in Soviet agricultural organization. The decree called for the agricultural management agencies to "organize within the shortest possible periods the transfer of all production subunits of agricultural, food processing and other enterprises to . . . the collective contract," that is, to complete the implementation of the brigade contract campaign. "Depending on the specific conditions of production," the decision also permitted sovkhozy and recommended that kolkhozy "use the family and individual contract in crop growing and animal husbandry as one of the forms of the collective contract" (CPSU Central Committee 1986a). It was also hedged with a requirement that pay be calculated as for any other brigade-contract collective using the whole complex apparatus of Soviet farm bookkeeping; thus this grudging permission allowed quiet experimentation but hardly offered the ringing endorsement needed to start a full-scale innovation campaign. For most of 1986, the press continued to beat the drums for the *brigadnyi podriad*, but little attention was paid to the family and individual contract.

A potentially more significant sign of change in agricultural policy was the joint party-state decision to suspend active preparation to build the massive water works needed to divert a portion of the flow of Siberian rivers to the south released in August 1986. This project, endorsed by the Central Committee during Konstantin Chernenko's brief leadership, continued the Brezhnev era line of massive investments rather than reorganization in order to increase agricultural output. The resolution provided that the investment should be diverted to the Russian Non-Black Earth Zone and the Volga region, and ordered that better water-use practices and conservation be instituted to cut water use by at least 10 percent by 1990 in the areas that would have received the Siberian water (CPSU Central Committee 1986b. Also see Darst 1988, and Micklin and Bond 1988). Although this resolution did not absolutely kill the diversion project, it marked an important stage in Gorbachev's reforms both because portions of the intelligentsia vocally participated in reopening the question and were allowed to claim some of the credit for ending the project and because the most visible symbol of the old policy of unlimited investment rather than economic and administrative reorganization had been stopped.

The family contract reappeared only after agricultural work was over for 1986. In November, a *Pravda* editorial noted the particular advantages of families taking on a brigade contract:

> Families are more and more frequently transferring to the accord system. Family livestock farms *(fermy)* are successfully operating in Estonia, the Moscow area, and a number of other regions. At times this is preferable: Many problems of organization, accounting, and wages are more simply solved in such collectives. Productivity is higher, discipline is stronger, the relation between earnings and final results is closer.

The editorial continued by explicitly approving individual contracts:

> Can a person take an individual contract? This initiative too should not be scorned, not even the services of people who labor on an accord contract when not working at their primary job. The main thing is to rely on khozraschet to eliminate the unearned ruble. The family and individual contract must have a firm legal basis ("Byt' zemli khoziainom" 1986).

Published only a week before the USSR Law on Individual Enterprise was adopted, this *Pravda* leader reaffirmed that brigade contracts should be made with families and individuals. A CPSU Central Committee resolution published in December made the party's approval of family farming even more explicit, calling for a "decisive transfer to new methods of management." The agricultural management and rural party apparatus was "by all means to develop the through and family contracts" (CPSU Central Committee 1986c). A "through" *(skvoznoi)* contract is one under which the same group is responsible for the whole production cycle, which means here the whole agricultural year.

In January 1987, CPSU agriculture secretary Viktor Nikonov reported at a Central Committee conference devoted to implementation of the December resolution that some eleven million people were working on agricultural collective contracts. They had charge of three-quarters of the country's plowland and 60 percent of its productive livestock. At the same time, "the family contract is widely distributed through all regions of the country" (*Pravda,* Jan. 25, 1987, p. 1). Yegor Ligachev's speech at the same conference helped to explain why the family contract had come back into favor. The agricultural sector produced the basic and most important consumer good, food. Yet despite the good 1986 harvest, deliveries to all-union food stocks were being reduced. The Ukraine, historically the country's breadbasket, had developed a negative grain balance, using more than it produced. Hard-currency grain imports needed to be curtailed. Dairy herd productivity in 1985 was at the same level as 1970 (*Pravda,* Jan. 25, 1987, p. 2). Although Ligachev did not mention the family contract, the need to introduce reforms which would provide real incentives to increase production and reduce inputs per unit of output on the farms was clearly stated. Citing Academician Tat'iana Zaslavskaia's well-known article, Ligachev argued that the "human factor," restoring initiative to the farmers, was the paramount requirement for a solution to the country's food problems. Particularly in crops which demanded a great deal of manual labor such as fruits and vegetables, Nikonov said, the family and individual contract had great potential.

The brigade contract campaign now began to focus on family and individual contracts. In June 1987, when the Central Committee met to consider a program for overall economic reform, the general secretary devoted one long passage of his report to the economic effectiveness of brigade contracts, drawing almost all his examples from contracting families. He also praised "Intensive Labor Collectives" (KITy), citing in particular the example of two brothers on a Novosibirsk farm who had increased production severalfold "O zadachakh . . . " 1987).

In August 1987, the general secretary visited a model sovkhoz outside Moscow. In his published remarks, he commented that allowing people to take responsibility for their own work, freeing them from the farm management's minute control, often had incredible results in the farm management's minute control, often had incredible results in increasing productivity and cutting costs. These effects were best and most quickly apparent in small groups, and that explained why "the family contract has gone well for us." Soviet farmers could be trusted to work better, wanted to work better, and should be paid for what they had done. Such initiative represented real socialism:

> From the example of collective contracts and family livestock *fermy* you have, certainly, come to feel how . . . our people want, hunger, not just to earn more—there is such a desire and it's understandable—but to earn honestly. They don't want to rip off the state, but to earn. Isn't this really a socialist desire? Completely socialist. So there shouldn't be any limitations—everything that a person earns must be given to him. You mustn't permit someone to be paid without having earned it. This is socialism.

The limitations, of course, were enforced by the agricultural managers, the administrators in charge of the wages budget and the reports. Gorbachev's comments not only attempted to redefine socialism in terms of wage differentials but implicitly attacked the whole management system. New forms of organization and incentives had come to the fore in the countryside. Soviet farmers had matured. They no longer needed the "petty tutelage" of their managers but could be trusted to work, and earn, and feed the country on their own.

Gorbachev asked one of the farm's workers if his contract collective wouldn't do even better if it had the land leased (perhaps the first time he used the word *arenda* in this sense). He was not advocating the abolition of the kolkhozy and sovkhozy. But because of their sheer size and large work groups, they were somewhat removed from the land. Now, the general secretary said:

> Within the framework of those kolkhozy and sovkhozy, through the collective and family contracts, through the *arendnyi podriad*, we must assure a connection with individual interests. And then we will unite the advantages of large collective farms with one's individual interest.

These changes were to be accomplished, he added, within two or three years. All that was needed was belief and intelligent work. The general secretary also reported that he and his Politburo colleagues had agreed that a Central Committee plenum would be convoked to deal with agrarian policy ("Perestroika izmeriaetsia . . ." 1987).

A month later, the party Central Committee ordered the completion of the transition to *podriad* labor organization and the general use of the family and individual contracts as well as the *arendnyi podriad:*

> Party committees and Soviet and economic agencies . . . are to give every support to production collectives that take means of production on *arenda* for long periods (10 to 15 years) and act as true masters of the land. The attention of Party, Soviet and economic officials has been called to existing instances of an incorrect, prejudiced attitude toward family and individual contracts and to the underestimation of their great potential. Officials have been instructed to take effective measures for the wide use of these forms of organization (CPSU Central Committee, 1987).

The resolution's timing gave officials the winter off-season to implement the decision. Since leasing land to individuals was still technically illegal, this was a case where party decisions were clearly superior to mere law.[10] This contradiction graphically demonstrated the urgency with which the Soviet leadership had decided to implement the leasing solution to the food problem, and so the seriousness of the food situation itself.

In January 1988, a draft of a new model kolkhoz charter appeared ("Proekt primernyi . . ." 1988). Since the kolkhoz charter specifies the kinds of work groups which can legally be used on the farm and had prohibited the leasing of land, a charter change was needed to legalize the lease.

At the Congress of Kolkhozniks which met in March to discuss the new Charter, Gorbachev advanced a radical proposal to substitute voluntary cooperatives for the bureaucratic agencies which had administered the Soviet countryside since collectivization. The kolkhozy and sovkhozy themselves should become profit-oriented "cooperatives of independent primary work groups," or "cooperatives of cooperatives" ("Potentsial kooperatsii . . ." 1988). In place of the cumbersome and costly apparatus of managers, accountants, and supervisors, a small management cooperative might run the farm's affairs, on a model urged by Lenin Agricultural Academy president Aleksandr Nikonov (and similar to experiments conducted in Kazakhstan by Ivan Khudenko in the 1960s which were closed down on Brezhnev's orders).

The Congress put off final passage of the new Charter until the Law on Cooperatives was finalized, however. Although the press continued to urge general adoption of the *arendnyi podriad* and reports of conversion of farms to "cooperatives of cooperatives" began to appear (Fomin 1988), the drive to transform the countryside was overshadowed by the political events leading up the Nineteenth Party Conference.

The most obvious turning point of early 1988 was the surge of elite conflict surrounding the "Andreeva letter" (Andreeva 1988; see also Chiesa 1988 and Tatu 1988). Echoing a demand in a January issue of the party theoretical journal *Kommunist* for a return to Stalinist relationships with the countryside when food prices were low and staples were available (Khabarova 1988), Andreeva defended the existing kolkhoz order as part of her general defense of Stalin, the party's history, and the party apparatus. The coincidence of Gorbachev's espousal of radically restructuring Soviet agricultural institutions and a movement of almost open opposition to perestroika emphasizes how important the existing kolkhoz system is as a component in the whole command economy.

As the country waited for the results of the Party Conference, even a Central Committee conference on the introduction of the lease in late May did little to increase momentum for reform. The general secretary demanded that introduction of the lease be wholesale *(sploshnaia)*, as collectivization was, but without its excesses ("Arendnyi podriad—kratchaishii . . ." 1988). By May, of course, work groups were organized for the year. Despite claims that the number of leasing collectives soared in 1988, there is good reason to think that most of the "changes" were limited to the reports.

Gosagroprom approved national recommendations for the *arendnyi podriad* in August 1988. Following the September 1988 Central Committee plenum which retired another group of conservative leaders, a further series of meetings on the *arenda* and related subjects were held under the auspices of the Central Committee in October and November (see Whitlock 1988). One of the gatherings discussed the work of the Orel oblast party committee in introducing the lease. (A year later, Orel first secretary Yegor Stroev replaced Viktor Nikonov, who was apparently less than enthusiastic over Gorbachev's agrarian policy, in the CPSU secretariat.)

The general secretary proposed restructuring the kolkhozy and sovkhozy, and the party-state apparatus which administered them, without doing away with the whole system. But by December 1988, some of the more radical agricultural economists were calling for the abolition of the whole kolkhoz system and a shift to agriculture based purely on individual peasants and small cooperatives. In a wide-ranging round table published in *Izvestiia,* Vladimir Bashmachnikov, a "konsul'tant" to the Economics Department of the CPSU Central Committee, argued that for leasing to work, the peasant must be made to feel the master of the land, the real "owner" *(vladel'ets)* of the means of production. Five conditions are needed for this transformation:

• freedom to choose the kind of economic activity in which the individual farmer will engage in order to do what is profitable for the market;

• independence in the organization of production;

• the right to freely choose partners in economic activity, to cooperate with whom he will in production and marketing;

• his own distribution of finished products, realized through channels he has chosen and at prices acceptable to consumer and producer; and

• the right to dispose of his income.

These conditions, observed Vladimir Tikhonov, another participant in the round table, are impossible in a system where farm organization and procurement are centrally dictated. The lessees must have the right to function outside of the framework of the collective farm, in free cooperatives, if the reform is to work (Abakumov and Gavrichkin 1988).

This forthright call for the abolition of the kolkhozy was not publicly acceptable to any of the Soviet leadership. Two weeks later, at a conference in the CPSU Central Committee, Gosagroprom chairman Murakhovskii harshly criticized people who called for the abolition of the collective farms, and Tikhonov was forced to deny he had meant that.[11] At almost the same time, Central Committee Agricultural Commission Chairman Ligachev praised a group of lessees in Saratov who said they could not get along without the kolkhoz.

The plenum on agrarian policy originally announced by Gorbachev in August 1987 finally met in March 1989. At the plenum, Gorbachev called for coexistence of the collective farms and the new cooperatives, as well as early finalization of a law on the lease which would legalize the *arendnyi podriad* as well as individual and cooperative leasing. Pending preparation of a law on the *arenda,* the Supreme Soviet Presidium issued an *ukaz* to set legal guidelines in April. An accompany-ing Council of Ministers resolution promised (not for the first time in post-Stalin Soviet history) that plans would be stable for an entire five-year plan and communicated to them in advance, that farms were free to dispose of above-plan produce as they wished, and guaranteed them independence in management decisions. The resolution also or-dered an end to piece-work payment, requiring that wages funds be drawn from the farm's profit after costs had been met and tied directly to final results of production ("Postanovlenie . . ." 1989). This provi-sion had the effect of putting all farms on a profit-and-loss *(khozraschet)* basis. However, its effectiveness will depend on the state's credit policy, since similar attempts to demand that all farms be profitable in the past were circumvented by obtaining bank loans to pay immediate expenses which were then obligingly written off.

High politics again eclipsed agrarian issues after the March plenum. Nationalities' unrest and wrangling about the new state structure occu-pied the summer and fall of 1989 as the Congress of People's Deputies struggled to define itself and debated ways to solve the growing Soviet economic crisis. A USSR Law on Leasing adopted in late November 1989 superseded the April Supreme Soviet Presidium *ukaz*. But pas-sage of a final law on land and an accompanying law on property has been delayed until early 1990, and perhaps later than that.

Political Issues

Because they challenge the received wisdom of the Stalinist system, the politics of the family and lease contracts are complex. At the elite level, introduction of the earlier brigade contract was clearly a return to an old dispute about the relative merits of further increasing agriculture's share of total state investment or reorganization to use existing investment more productively.[12] The river diversion plan con-tinued the Brezhnev-era strategy of higher investments in land recla-mation and farm equipment which successfully bought the former general secretary support from regional officials fearful of reorganiza-tion and heavy-industrial and defense ministries who would benefit from expanded production. This dispute was, for the moment, settled by the 1986 decision to stop work on the diversion of Siberian rivers to Central Asia, redefining the political cleavage between reorganization and investment.

The investment or reorganization controversy has shifted to a dispute about the effectiveness of investment in infrastructure and food processing industry. Ligachev, former Central Committee Secretary Nikonov, and Prime Minister Nikolai Ryzhkov constantly demand that agricultural infrastructure be improved and food processing facilities upgraded (while saying little about family farming and especially not about new forms of property and land leasing). A major program to achieve these purposes was announced in late 1987. It seems that the entire Soviet elite agrees on the necessity of these measures. But they do not all agree that investment is enough without reorganization as well.

Three alternative policies emerge from the family lease campaign. Should the *arendnyi podriad* be limited to within the farms, essentially leaving the farm management and structure intact? Or should the kolkhozy and sovkhozy be radically restructured into cooperatives of cooperatives? Or must they be done away with altogether? Ligachev is careful to praise the intrafarm lease, but he implies that with the *arendnyi podriad* and better management, the existing system is quite capable of solving the food problem. Gorbachev, by contrast, talks about reorganizing the farms and a variety of forms of property in the countryside. When pushed hard, he has always denied any intention of eliminating the kolkhozy and sovkhozy, but he seems willing to accept the consequences of a fundamentally reorganized countryside in which kolkhozy and sovkhozy do not dominate. Both leaders reject the alternative of simply abolishing state and collective farms.

Gorbachev and Ligachev have different reasons for resisting complete decollectivization, however. Their dispute involves the ideological underpinnings of the system. Gorbachev is willing to throw out the whole Stalinist legacy, which means admitting that all of collectivization was an error—although the farms can and should be rebuilt to utilize their real economies of scale within a truly cooperative framework. Ligachev is not willing to reject all of Soviet history, especially collectivization. Gorbachev apparently believes that the peasantry can be trusted to support the regime even without the massive control apparatus represented by the farms, and suggests that the party should change its role in society to one of selecting and training political leaders rather than explicitly determining all national policy. Ligachev has not said so plainly, but he clearly assumes that the party's role in Soviet society depends on its political and administrative apparatus, and doubts that the party can hold power without it.

Once it is recognized that the argument about the *arenda* is really about the party's role in society, the coincidence of debates about collectivization with the late 1987 decision to generally implement the *arendnyi podriad* seems far from accidental.[13] For Nina Andreeva, as well as Ligachev and perhaps many other Communists, the kolkhoz system is not so much an economic mechanism as a symbol of party authority. Altering or abolishing the institution threatens not so much agriculture as the party's right to rule.

The lease is also clearly controversial among the middle level of the Soviet elite, the government and party officials charged with making particular industries or regions operate as they should. These members of the broader elite are important political players because of their power as members or candidate members of the Central Committee who can bring down a general secretary when the conditions are right. They are also the cadres who must implement any top-level decision, and they can frequently frustrate any reform if they so choose. As a result, their positions are important political stakes, and the processes of building a personal and factional power base among the middle elites by Politburo barons and picking off clients of one's opponents are much of the day-to-day stuff of Soviet politics.

Introduction of leasing has so far varied a great deal from region to region. Belgorod, Orel, and Kostroma oblasts and Krasnodar and Stavropol' krais seem to be most active in introducing the *arendnyi podriad* in the Russian Republic, for instance. Interestingly, Belgorod was the model for the brigade contract, while it and the others were all leaders in the introduction of mechanized and complex mechanized links in the late 1950s and 1960s.[14] Many other areas have been criticized for their half-hearted implementation of the new ideas. One likely reason for this variability is the factional inclination of the regional party first secretary. However, their current success in fulfilling plans, the availability of farmers and farm managers willing to try the new forms as an experiment, and perhaps even the weather may also help to explain the variability of use of the new forms.

On the farms themselves, reaction to the new lease arrangements seems mixed. Farm managers and specialists, unable to cope with new conditions and fearful of a loss of power and position, often treat the lessees extremely cavalierly. When one division of a Karaganda sovkhoz decided to break from the farm and become a cooperative, the division head had to get permission from the raikom first secretary before the cooperative could have its own bank account. Then the farm demanded that it pay off 500,000 rubles for cows and calves during its first year, charged it 20,000 rubles for a duplex apartment building with no utilities put up some forty years earlier, and took lease payments on equipment. As the reporter commented, these conditions amounted to "debt slavery" *("usloviia . . . kabal'nye")* (Ryzhkov 1989).

There are fewer stories of opposition from the farms' manual workers, but it clearly must exist. If the *arenda* is successful, not only will many workers become redundant, but a threat to the kolkhozy also implies a threat to the pensions and side benefits that many of the rural population can draw from them. Unemployment can, of course, be handled by creating sideline enterprises or by open unemployment payments. The benefits farms give their elderly and non-able-bodied workers now are hardly generous. But so far little attention has been paid to problems of easing the transition. In the meantime, manual workers and pensioners are a ready-made captive constituency for manipulation by farm specialists and managers who want to defend their own positions.

Conversion to real leasing requires that something be done with the many farms which are unprofitable. Advocates of leasing often suggest that just introducing the new system and ridding the farms of their vast superstructure of unproductive managerial and accounting personnel will make most farms profitable, but this is almost certainly not enough. Extremely unprofitable farms may still be attached to stronger neighboring farms, the traditional way to solve the problem of a losing operation. However, Gorbachev has proposed that unprofitable farms should become subsidiaries of profitable industrial enterprises. By April 1989, some 140 unprofitable farms had been converted to "agroshops" (*Pravda*, April 2, 1989, p. 2).

Conclusions

The campaign for the lease contract and family farming is a central element of perestroika. As such, it is bound up with a number of other issues. Reexamination of the history of collectivization is a way of guaranteeing that successful lessees need not fear that they will someday be "dekulakized." Reform of agricultural prices and elimination of state subsidies for production of many items will fundamentally affect the leaseholders' financial position and their contracts with the farms (it is even possible to imagine lessees uniting to defend the subsidy system, although so far they have been generally kept from sharing its abundance by one-sided contracts which allow the farms to take much of their profits). Creation of a "socialist state of laws," implying an independent judiciary able to make its decisions apply to the state as well as its citizens, also offers lessees a guarantee that they will be allowed to retain their new farms, as well as creating new state institutions capable of enforcing their rights and implementing the new innovations in the countryside. Most importantly, however, is a new law on land, which would establish their property rights. Long-term use rights on the model of the *postoiannoe pol'zovanie* held by kolkhozy might be enough, and this limited property right seems to be what Gorbachev's discussion of various forms of property in the countryside envisions.

Others, however, suggest that the land must be sold to the peasants. Although in theory this seems to be an attractive way to sop up some of the excess money in circulation, there appear to be few peasants who support this idea. Probably, as Anatolii Anan'ev suggests, the peasants resist paying for the land because they already have done so, first during the emancipation and then during the Civil War and World War II (*Pravda,* June 15, 1989, p. 3). One of the greatest obstacles to leasing may be in this resistance of the peasant to once again pay for what he believes to be his own by right anyway.

Despite its problems, the leasing campaign seems likely to bring about real change. Unlike previous attempts to alter agricultural work and give the peasants new incentives in order to increase production, this time around the regime acknowledges that more than just the organization and pay arrangements within the farms must be changed. The leadership's own cries of "crisis" make it more important for the regime to succeed in increasing food supplies.

However, the difficulties of carrying out successful reform within a political and governmental structure attuned to short-term, high-intensity, but highly routinized campaigns means that the leasing drive will not be widely adopted or bring about fundamental changes quickly. Other political instruments, both new institutions to represent social interests in the state such as the Congress of People's Deputies and non-state organizations capable of uniting farmers such as the new

Union of Peasant Farmers and Agricultural Cooperatives of Russia founded in the summer of 1989 will be needed to give peasants mechanisms to defend themselves against the apparatus and its allies and change the balance of power in the countryside. Even then, conservative elements may be able to use some of the new forms to defend existing arrangements.[15]

Whether or not a countryside covered with a patchwork of individual peasant farms, rural production cooperatives, kolkhozy, and sovkhozy is still "collectivized" is a semantic problem. But for the leaders who began it and the party-state administrative apparatus, the current campaign to introduce the family and lease contract may be almost as dangerous if it succeeds as if it fails.

Notes

1. Preliminary work on this paper was done as a Title VIII Visiting Scholar at the Hoover Institution, Stanford University. Financial support from the Academic Council of Hamilton College is also gratefully acknowledged.

2. The Kolkhoz Model Charter adopted at the Second Congress of Kolkhozniki-udarniki in 1935 standardized kolkhoz organization. Until 1956, farms were required to adopt the entire charter absolutely unchanged. Although they then received the right to adapt certain provisions to local circumstances, most farms in fact seem not to have done so. The model charter was revised at the Third Congress of Kolkhozniki in 1969 and again in 1988 (see below).

3. Although the kolkhoz is formally a cooperative farm, while the sovkhoz is directly state-owned, the practical differences between the two have been very slight in practice, especially since guaranteed wages were introduced on the kolkhozy in the mid-1960s.

4. I make this argument more fully in my "To Be 'Master of the Land': The Politics of Reform in the Soviet Countryside, 1935–1989," unpublished manuscript.

5. Such "recommendations" are actually orders for organizations subordinate to the ministry which issues them. The *arendnyi podriad* recommendations, "rekomendatsii po organizatsii arendnykh otnoshenii sel'skokhoziaistvennom proizvodstve," were published in part in *Sel'skaia zhizn'* (August 27, 1988), p. 1, and in full in *APK: Ekonomika upravlenie*, no. 12 (December 1988), pp. 93–99.

6. "Ukaz Prezidiuma . . ." (1989); "Osnovyi . . ." (1989). The translation in FBIS-SOV (December 12, 1989), pp. 60–67, renders "arendnyi podriad" as "contract leasing."

7. The April 1989 *ukaz* allowed farmers working on *arendnyi podriad* to go to court if permitted by the relevant legislation. The December law does not mention a right of appeal to court for holders of an *arendnyi podriad*, although it provides it for *arendatory* in general.

8. The April 1989 Supreme Soviet *ukaz* says that property which belongs to the state may not be bought by the *arendator*. The December law specifically

provides that funds from purchases of state property by leasing collectives go into the state budget, eliminating that restriction.

9. For analyses of the brigade contract campaign, see Gagnon (1987), and chapter eleven of my "To Be 'Master of the Land.'"

10. In an interview with a responsible official of the Latvian Gosagroprom in March 1988, I commented that the *arendnyi podriad* was technically illegal since it contravened the basic land law in force. My interlocutor agreed, but added that they were introducing the lease contract on the strength of Gorbachev's speech (presumably the August one cited here) anyway.

11. The meeting is reported in *Pravda* (January 15, 1989). Murakhovskii repeated his criticisms at the March plenum, without mentioning Tikhonov by name, saying that among other people, "some economists, including VASKhNIL academicians," were confused on this point. *Pravda* (March 17, 1989), p. 2.

12. This analysis was suggested by Werner Hahn (1972).

13. On the historical debate, see Sherlock 1988; Davies 1989; and Sherlock and Tolz 1989.

14. The intensive-labor collectives which appeared during the transition from the brigade to the *arendnyi podriad* were most prominent in Novosibirsk oblast', a province then run by a long-time associate and rumored relative of Ligachev, A. P. Filatov. Like the brigade contracts, the KITy posed no threat to the farms as such.

15. This seems to be the underlying motive in several recent threats to withhold production from state procurement agencies unless prices for industrial goods sold to the farms are lowered.

References

Abakumov, Igor' and Valerii Gavrichkin (1988). "Budet li u zemli khoziain?" *Izvestiia* (December 29): 2.

Andreeva, Nina (1988). "Pis'mo v redaktsiiu prepodavatelia leningradskogo vuza: Ne mogu postupat'sia printsipami." *Sovetskaia Rossiia* (March 13): 3.

"Arendnyi podriad—kratchaishii put' k prodovol'stvennomu dostatku: Vstrecha v tsentral'nom komitete KPSS." *Pravda* (May 15, 1988): 1–4.

"Byt' zemli khoziainom." *Pravda* (November 11, 1986): 1.

Chiesa, Giuletto (1988). "Secret Story Behind Anti-Gorbachev Manifesto." *L'Unita* (May 23), as translated in FBIS-SOV (May 31, 1988): 55–58.

CPSU Central Committee (1986a) and USSR Council of Ministers Resolution. "O dal'neishem sovershenstvovanii ekonomicheskogo mekhanizma khoziaistvovaniia v agropromyshlennom komplekse strany." *Pravda* (March 29): 1–2.

CPSU Central Committee (1986b) and USSR Council of Ministers Resolution. "O prekrashchenii rabot po perebroske chasti stoka severnykh i Sibirskikh rek." *Pravda* (August 20): 1.

CPSU Central Committee (1986c) Resolution. "O neotlozhnykh merakh po povysheniiu proizvoditel'nosti truda v sel'skom khoziaistve na osnove vnedreniia ratsional'nykh form ego organizatsii i khozrascheta." *Pravda* (December 18): 1.

CPSU Central Committee (1987) Resolution. "O neotlozhnykh merakh po uskoreniiu resheniia prodovol'stvennogo voprosa v sootvetstvii s ustanovkami iiun'skogo (1987 g.) plenuma TsK KPSS." *Pravda* (September 25, 1987): 1–2.

Darst, Robert G., Jr. (1988). "Environmentalism in the USSR: The Opposition to the River Diversion Projects." *Soviet Economy* 4, no. 3, pp. 223–52.

Davies, R.W. (1989). *Soviet History in the Gorbachev Revolution.* Bloomington: Indiana University Press.

Fomin, Vladimir (1988). "Po vsem krest'ianskim pravilam." *Don,* no. 7 (July): 127–33.

Gagnon, V.P., Jr. (1987). "Gorbachev and the Brigade Contract." *Soviet Studies.*

Hahn, Werner (1972). *The Politics of Soviet Agriculture, 1960–1970.* Baltimore: Johns Hopkins University Press.

Khabarova, T.M. (1988). "O sotsialisticheskoi modifikatsii stoimosti." *Kommunist,* no. 1 (January): 97–100.

Micklin, Philip P., and Andrew R. Bond (1988). "Reflections on Environmentalism and the River Diversion Projects." *Soviet Economy* 4, no. 3: 253–74.

Nikitin, A. (1989). "Diskussionnaia tribuna: Filosofiia arendy." *Pravda* (December 7): 2.

"O zadachakh partii po korennoi perestroike upravleniia ekonomikoi: Doklad General'nogo Sekretaria TsK KPSS M. S. Gorbacheva na Plenume TsK KPSS 25 iiunia 1987 goda." *Pravda* (June 26, 1987): 2.

"Ob agrarnoi politike KPSS v sovremennykh usloviiakh: Doklad General'nogo Sekretaria TsK KPSS M. S. Gorbacheva na Plenume TsK KPSS 15 marta 1989 goda." *Pravda* (March 16, 1989): 2.

"Orenburgskie mekhanizatory prizyvaiut khleborobskie dinastii pravernyt sorevnovanie: Na zhatvu—semeinym ekipazhem." *Sovetskaia Rossiia* (June 24, 1989): 1.

"Osnovyi zakonodatel'stva Soiuza SSSR i soiuznykh respublik: Ob arende." *Izvestiia* (December 1, 1989): 3. The translation in FBIS-SOV (December 12, 1989): 60–67, renders *arendnyi podriad* as "contract leasing."

"Perestroika izmeriaetsia delami: Vstrechi M. S. Gorbacheva s sel'skimi truzhenikami podmoskov'ia." *Pravda* (August 6, 1987): 1–2.

"Politicheskii doklad tsentral'nogo komiteta KPSS." In *XXVII s''ezd kommunisticheskoi partii sovetskogo soiuza: stenograficheskii otchet,* pp. 23–121. Moscow: Izdatel'stvo politicheskoi literatury, 1986.

"Polozhenie o planirovanii, uchete i otchetnosti pri arendnykh otnosheniiakh v sel'skokhoziaistvennom proizvodstve." *APK: Ekonomika, upravlenie,* no. 2 (February 1989): 113–24.

"Postanovlenie Soveta Ministrov SSSR ot 5 aprelia 1989 g.: O korennoi perestroike ekonomicheskikh otnoshenii i upravleniia v agropromyshlennom komplekse strany." *Pravda* (April 12, 1989): 2.

"Potentsial kooperatsii—delu perestroiki. Vystuplenie general'nogo sekretaria TsK KPSS M. S. Gorbacheva." In *Chetvertyi vsesoiuznyi s''ezd kolkhoznikov: stenograficheskii otchet,* pp. 21–50. Moscow: VO "Agropromizdat," 1988.

Pravda, January 25, 1987; January 15, 1989; March 17, 1989; April 2, 1989; June 15, 1989.

"Proekt primernyi ustav kolkhoza." *Sel'skaia zhizn'* (January 10, 1988): 1–2.

"Rekomendatsii po organizatsii arendnykh otnoshenii v sel'skokhoziaistvennom proizvodstve." Published in part in *Sel'skaia zhizn'* (August 27, 1988): 1; and in full in *APK: Ekonomika, upravlenie,* no. 12 (December, 1988): 93–99.

Ryzhkov, V. (1989). "Osilit khoziain: kooperativ—dobryi partner pokupatelia." *Pravda* (June 9): 5.

Shabanov, Iu. (1976). "Slovo laureatam gosudarstvennoi premii SSSR: Synov'ia ukhodiat v pole." *Sel'skoe khoziaistvo Rossii,* no. 2 (February): 6–7.

Sherlock, Thomas (1988). "Politics and History under Gorbachev." *Problems of Communism* 37, no. 3–4: 16–43.

Sherlock, Thomas, and Vera Tolz (1989). "Debates over Number of Stalin's Victims in the USSR and in the West." *Radio Liberty Research* 409/89 (August 23).

Shmelev, G. *Pravda* (March 20, 1986): 1, as translated in FBIS-SOV (March 24, 1986).

Sokolov, Vladimir (1988). "Zona molchaniia." *Literaturnaia gazeta,* no. 3 (January 20): 13.

Tatu (1988). "19th CPSU Conference." *Problems of Communism* 37, no. 3–4: 1–15.

"Ukaz Prezidiuma Verkhovnogo Soveta SSSR: Ob arende i arendnykh otnosheniiakh v sssr." *Pravda* (April 9, 1989): 2.

USSR Council of Ministers (1989). "O korennoi perestroike ekonomicheskikh otnoshenii i upravleniia v agropromyshlennom komplekse strany." *Pravda* (April 12): 2.

Uzun, V.Ia. (1987). "Ekonomika i organizatsiia: melkogruppovaia i semeinaia formy organizatsii proizvodstva i truda v sel'skom khoziaistve." *Vestnik sel'skokhoziaistvennoi nauki,* no. 6 (June): 5.

Van Atta, D. (1989). "To Be 'Master of the Land': The Politics of Reform in the Soviet Countryside, 1935–1989." Unpublished manuscript.

Whitlock, Eric (1988). "Face to the Countryside: Further Developments in Soviet Agricultural Policy." *Radio Liberty Research* 515/88 (November 15).

D. GALE JOHNSON

Possible Impacts of Agricultural
Trade Liberalization on the USSR

If it is assumed that the USSR does not modify its national economic policies, including its agricultural policies, it is quite obvious that significant success in liberalizing agricultural trade will adversely affect the USSR. There are two reasons for this conclusion. First, the USSR is a large net importer of temperate zone agricultural products, and, second, trade liberalization would result in significant increases in the prices of several of the agricultural products that the USSR imports. Under the assumptions made, the USSR would be faced with higher prices for its agricultural imports. It might also receive higher prices for its exports of agricultural products, but such exports are quite small. The value of USSR agricultural exports averaged $2.4 billion for 1985–87 while imports averaged $16.1 billion (ERS 1989). Consequently, the higher international market prices for agricultural products would increase the value of exports very little compared to the increase in the import bill.

Price Effects of Trade Liberalization

There have been several studies of the effects of trade liberalization for agricultural products upon the international market prices of farm products. The results vary from study to study, primarily because they use different base periods and do not assume that trade liberalization occurs in the same combination of countries. Trade liberalization for agricultural products is concerned as much with reducing governmental interventions in domestic markets as it is in eliminating overt trade barriers and subsidies at the border. In the case of agriculture, trade barriers are primarily the consequence of governmental interventions in the domestic markets for farm products. When governments establish price supports or attempt to stabilize domestic prices, trade must

The author is Professor Emeritus at the University of Chicago.

be regulated if the government is to meet its domestic price objective with acceptable demands upon the treasury. Price stability even at a level that provides little or no long-run protection requires either import controls or export subsidies. Without such devices and with free trade, the domestic prices would vary with international market prices as imports and exports occurred in response to any differences in the two prices.

This is not the place to present the detailed results of the considerable number of studies that have been made. For our purposes a rather rough summary will suffice.

The studies based on periods during the late 1970s or early 1980s indicated rather modest effects of trade liberalization upon international market prices for grains and sugar. The reason was that during those years the degrees of protection of such products in the industrial market economies were relatively small. These studies (Parikh 1988; OECD 1987) projected international market price increases of 5 to 10 percent for grains and sugar from full liberalization of trade in agriculture by the industrial market economies. A third study by Tyers gave similar results. The three studies projected much larger price increases for dairy products of 40 to 80 percent and increases of 18 to 25 percent for ruminant meat (primarily beef).

However, studies based on the protection levels of the mid-1980s showed much greater price increases from trade liberalization since the rate of protection was much higher in the mid-1980s than in the earlier years referred to above. Tyers and Anderson (1988) projected price increases for 1995 of 25 percent for wheat, 18 percent for rice, 43 percent for ruminant meat, 10 percent for nonruminant meat, 95 percent for dairy products, and 22 percent for sugar for a weighted average of 30 percent. Roningen and Dixit (1988) used a model to project the effects of trade liberalization based on the levels of protection that prevailed in 1986/87. Their model, as well as the one used by Tyers and Anderson, included the effects of abandoning the supply management programs of the United States upon farm output and world market prices. Their projection was that the average of international market prices would increase by 19 percent, with the largest increase being 50 percent for dairy products and the smallest increase being 7 percent for oilseeds. Grain prices were projected to increase by 23 percent for feed grains to 30 percent for wheat.

It may be noted that there have been significant increases in international market prices for many farm products since the low points in 1986 or 1986/87. The price increases have occurred primarily because of the reduction in the large stocks of cereals, dairy products, and meats since that time. The reduction in stocks reflected adjustments to the lower prices and to production shortfalls in 1988.

Effects on USSR Import Bill

At this point I shall compare the composition of the USSR agricultural import bill with the pattern of price increases. Based on the average imports by category for 1986 and 1987, and assuming that there would be no response in amounts imported to the increases in international market prices, the annual import bill would increase from $1.25 billion to $1.5 billion. This amount may seem to be a small effect, given the magnitude of the projected price increases, but given the composition of its imports, only 40 percent of USSR agricultural imports are of products whose prices would be significantly affected by trade liberalization *and* for which the price would increase to a level higher than called for by ongoing Soviet commitments. These include grains (18 percent), meat and animals (10 percent), oilseeds (5 percent), and vegetable oils (3 percent). Sugar accounted for 31 percent of the value of agricultural imports and trade liberalization would have a significant effect on world market prices. Why is sugar not included in the estimate of additional import cost? The reason is a simple one—the USSR now pays much more for its sugar relative to the world market price. The price, according to the U.S. Department of Agriculture, averaged somewhat more than $900 per metric ton in 1986 and 1987 (ERS 1989). In the last decade the highest annual average international market price has been on the order of $640 per ton (1980) and the lowest about $90 per ton (1985). The U.S. price support, as high as it is, is about $450 per ton and no one imagines the long-run world average price could exceed the U.S. price support level even though in the short run and for a brief period world sugar prices could exceed that level. Even though trade liberalization would increase sugar prices by a significant percentage, the market price would have no direct effect upon the Soviet import bill. There might be an indirect effect if there is an approximate formula that determines what the USSR pays for Cuban sugar which reflects the world market price.

While an increase in import costs for agricultural products of $1.25

billion to $1.5 billion cannot be ignored, it does not seem so large as to be insurmountable. By making some adjustments in the products imported in response to the changes in relative import prices some savings could be realized. For example, trade liberalization will increase the prices of feed grains less than food grains and oilseeds and oilmeals by less than either of the grains. Consequently, by changing the composition of imports it would be possible to achieve the same effects upon output or consumption at a lower import cost. For example, the same level of livestock production could be achieved by importing less feed grains and more oilseeds or oilmeals and in the process reduce the import bill below what it would be if no change were made in the composition of feed imports. This effect is over and above the savings that could be achieved by importing more oilseeds and less feed grains at existing prices since livestock rations in the USSR are significantly short on protein.

The above estimate of the effect of trade liberalization on the USSR import bill does not reflect the impact of the loss of preferential export treatment that the country has received as a result of the competitive export subsidy programs of the European Community (EC) and the United States. The EC and the U.S. have found the USSR to be a favorite dumping ground for their excess stocks of cereals and, in the case of the EC, butter. The USSR has gained from the rather misguided effort of the U.S. to increase the cost of the Common Agricultural Program by lowering the import prices in certain markets. The USSR has been one of those markets.

In 1987, before there had been a significant recovery from the low 1986 prices, the average U.S. export price of wheat was $94.40; during the same time period the price for wheat exported to the USSR was $80.97—a difference of about 15 percent. The export subsidy was much larger than implied by the price difference, presumably due to the differences in wheat quality. Perhaps a better indicator of the importance of the preferential treatment received by the USSR was that during 1987/88 the cost of the U.S. export subsidies on wheat sold to the USSR was $450 million and the average rate was $32 per ton, down from $42 the previous year. It may be noted that the EC exported about the same amount of wheat to the USSR as did the U.S., and EC exports are subsidized to provide at least the same import price, taking quality variables into account. Except perhaps for some high quality wheat from Canada, the other exporters to the USSR must match the

U.S. and EC prices. Consequently, the USSR benefits from the effects of the export subsidies on all of its wheat imports, regardless of the source.

If trade liberalization resulted in the abolition of the competitive export subsidies, the USSR agricultural import bill could increase by at least an additional $1 billion compared to the earlier figure. The projected price effects of trade liberalization did not include the elimination of export subsidies or, if such effects were included, it would have been only the average effect on world market prices and not the differential gain realized by a given importer.

What If?

What if the USSR also liberalized its trade in agriculture? Then the above projections of the impacts of trade liberalization would almost certainly be wide of the mark. Obviously, the assumption that agricultural trade was liberalized requires major reform of domestic policies and a ruble with a realistic value. I am assuming much more than a price reform that related domestic prices to world market prices. I would not argue that the ruble has to be convertible, but the correspondence between the official exchange rate and the equilibrium rate must be far closer than the current rate of $1.60 is to my estimate of the equilibrium rate of perhaps $0.30 to $0.50. The current black market rate is no more than $0.12.

I disagree with the viewpoint that the USSR does not have a long-run comparative advantage in agriculture. The present situation is so full of distortions that one cannot be sure of what agriculture's comparative advantage would be if the distortions were eliminated. The distortions include the inadequate state of the rural infrastructure, such as roads, shops and schools, the organizational structure of agriculture, the structure of incentives for workers, the rationing of most inputs by means other than price, and the governmental interventions in prices that encourage excess consumption of some products and discourage the production of most. If the equilibrium exchange rate were $0.30, most farm prices would be well below international market prices.

For example, the recent average price paid to collective farms for grain was approximately 170 rubles (ERS). If a ruble is worth $0.30, then the price is equal to $51 compared to U.S. prices for wheat in recent years of $120 to $140 per ton and $80–$120 for corn. Soviet import prices would be at least $20 per ton greater than these prices if there were no export subsidies.

Perhaps $0.30 is too low for the equilibrium rate. An indication of what the Soviet officials think the rate might be may be derived from the announcement made in July 1989 that farms who delivered more wheat than they did in 1981–85 would be paid the equivalent of 40 to 60 rubles per ton in foreign exchange. The 40 to 60 rubles is from 24 to 36 percent of the average ruble price received by Soviet farms; this implies an exchange rate of $0.37 to $0.56 per ruble. But even if the equilibrium rate is $0.50, farm prices for grains, oilseeds, cotton, and eggs are currently below external market prices and by a substantial percentage for oilseeds and eggs. Cattle and hog prices appear to be near world prices with a ruble value of $0.50 but below if the equilibrium rate is $0.30.

Earlier I noted that liberalization of domestic farm policies in the USSR would require much more than realigning farm prices with world market prices at a sustainable exchange rate. The liberalization would imply that farms produce in response to the prices of outputs and inputs and not to procurement plans promulgated from on high. Farm inputs would be freely imported and marketing institutions would be competitive rather than state monopsonies or monopolies. Implicit in the idea of liberalization is that the major agricultural institutions would either be abolished or substantially reformed. By major agricultural institutions I mean primarily the state and collective farms. If these institutions were retained, they should be transformed into true cooperatives that made decisions on the basis of the interests of their members or workers and not to meet the manifold and inconsistent criteria that are now established by planners and bureaucrats. The planning institutions should be prohibited from establishing procurement goals and no other governmental institution would be permitted to impose marketing plans upon agricultural producers. This would mean, at long last, that there was recognition by politicians and ideologues that farm people were capable of managing their own affairs and to do so in ways consistent with national interests if given the proper price signals.

I do not know how great that increase would be but the Chinese agricultural and rural reforms may give some indication of the order of magnitude. Based on personal observation I would say that the negative production effects of the distortions that now exist in Soviet agriculture are at least as large as what existed in China in 1978. A minimum estimate of the effects of the Chinese rural reforms on agricultural output was an increase of 20 percent (Lin 1987). Two other studies (McMillan, Whalley, and Li 1989; Wen 1989) give similar or greater estimates of the output effects of the Chinese reforms.

If there were a price reform of retail food prices that eliminated the subsidy component and if Soviet farm prices were at the world market levels, the quantities of meat and dairy products demanded might well be less than what are now being consumed. The state retail price of meat would approximately double if the ruble exchange rate were $0.50; if the exchange rate were as low as $0.30, the retail prices would need to more than double. These conclusions about retail prices assume that the price subsidies for meat would no longer exist. The consumption effects of such retail prices would depend upon how much further nominal wages are permitted to increase. However, increases in nominal wages greater than the increase in labor productivity would be reflected in a reduction in the foreign exchange value of the ruble. Thus if farm prices were related to world market prices, further nominal changes in wage incomes would not have much effect on the worker's short-run ability to purchase food if the Soviet economy were on a free trade basis.

But given the disequilibrium that now exists in the markets for meat and milk products, as well as in the markets for most items of daily consumption, it is perhaps idle to speculate about the level of consumption that would occur if farm product prices were at international market levels and there were a reasonable rate of exchange. What does seem apparent is that there would be three major factors affecting trade in agricultural products over a period of several years if the Soviet economy became a market economy with openness to the world economy. One factor would be the substantial increase in agricultural output; a second factor would be the consumption effects of significantly higher real prices for most food products and especially for meat and milk, and the third factor would be a significant increase in real incomes if there were successful reforms of the industrial, agricultural, and service sectors. The last factor may be the most speculative of the three, but it could also be the most important in determining the trade effects of economic liberalization. If real per capita incomes were to increase by 50 percent over a period of a decade, which seems within the realm of possibility, the shift in the demand for agricultural products would be substantial due to the relatively high income elasticities of demand. But I do not know if the net effect would be to increase the aggregate quantities of agricultural products consumed, given the increase in retail prices. Since I have gone this far in my speculation, I should give my conclusion, namely that in a market economy open to the world the Soviet Union would once again be a rather important exporter of agricultural products.

Exchange Rate for Tourists

After I had written the above speculations about the equilibrium exchange rate, the Soviet government announced on October 25, 1989, that the exchange rate for certain tourist transactions was to be approximately $0.16. This was a stunning action and it is not obvious what its full implications will be. But I do not believe that the equilibrium exchange rate could be as low as $0.16. Since I assume that most foreign tourists who come to the USSR will pay for their accommodations, food, and travel in convertible currency, the tourist exchange rate will only apply to the marginal expenditures of the tourist.

The major impact will be upon the Soviet citizen who wishes to travel abroad and who now will have to pay ten times as much in rubles for dollars or other hard currency than he or she did before. Consequently, it appears that this rate is more important as an indicator of boldness in economic policy and of possible things to come than will be its effects upon the economy. This change was apparently intended to be the first move toward rationalizing the ruble exchange rate.

Concluding Comments

If the current round of GATT negotiations is successful in eliminating most of the governmental intervention in agriculture in the industrial market economies, the short-run effect would be to increase the cost of Soviet agricultural imports. The combined effects of higher world market prices plus the elimination of export subsidies by the European Community and the United States could increase the import bill by about $2 billion. This assumes that no adjustments are made to the composition of imports; obviously the effect on the import bill could be reduced by importing less of products with the largest price increases and importing more of those with the smallest increases.

What is far more intriguing, but subject to enormous uncertainty, is what would occur if the Soviet economy underwent a major reform and emerged as a socialist market economy that was open to the world economy. Under this scenario, my hunch is that agriculture would have a significant comparative advantage in the Soviet Union and we would once again see net exports rather than very large net imports of agricultural products.

References

Economic Research Service (ERS) (1989). United States Department of Agriculture. *USSR Agriculture and Trade Report*, RS–89–1 (May).

Lin, Justin (1987). "Household Farm, Cooperative Farm, and Efficiency: Evidence from Rural De-Collectivization in China." Economic Growth Center, Yale University (March).

McMillan, John; John Whalley; and Li Jing Zu (1989). "The Impact of China's Economic Reforms on Agricultural Productivity Growth." *Journal of Political Economy* 97 (August).

Organization for Economic Cooperation and Development (1987). *National Policies and Agricultural Trade*. Paris: OECD.

Parikh, K. S.; G. Fischer; K. Frohberg; and O. Gulbrandsen (1988). *Towards Free Trade in Agriculture*. International Institute for Applied Systems Analysis (IIASA). Dordrecht: Martinus Nijhoff Publishers.

Tyers, Rod (1982). "Effects on ASEAN of Food Trade Liberalization in Industrial Countries." Paper presented to the Second Western Pacific Food Trade Workshop, Jakarta (August 22–23).

Tyers, Rod, and Kym Anderson (1988). "Liberalizing OECD Agricultural Policies in the Uruguay Round: Effects on Trade and Welfare." *Journal of Agricultural Economics* 30, no. 2 (May).

Wen, James (1989). "The Current Tenure System and Its Impact on Long Term Performance of Farming Sector: The Case of Modern China." Unpublished Ph.D. dissertation, Department of Economics, The University of Chicago.

MICHAEL MARRESE

Hungarian Agriculture
Lessons for the Soviet Union

Introduction

The idea that Soviet perestroika will not succeed without a radical reform of Soviet agrarian policy became painfully self-evident in 1989.[1] Rationing, food shortages, strikes, and increases in the percentage of family income that many families spend on food are all widespread phenomena in the Soviet Union today. At the same time, Soviet income distribution is worsening, inflation in retail prices reached new heights during the first six months of 1989, and there is a growing belief among a great portion of the Soviet population that the cooperative movement is corrupt.[2] Under these conditions, this paper addresses the issue of how Hungarian agricultural experience can provide insight into ways the Soviet Union can solve its agricultural problems.

This paper is organized as follows. The first section outlines the weaknesses in Soviet agriculture and the obstacles hindering the implementation of radical reform. The next section is devoted to the reasons why Hungary is, at first glance, an attractive example for the Soviet Union to follow, even though a closer examination uncovers the dangers embedded in this strategy. Next a summary of the evolution of Hungarian agricultural policy since 1965 is presented. We then examine the reasons that Hungarian experience has only limited applicability as well as the positive lessons that Hungary offers the Soviet Union.

Weaknesses in Soviet Agriculture
and Obstacles to Radical Reform

The clearest signs of the weaknesses of Soviet agriculture are: the commonplace food shortages; the 90-billion-ruble federal budget sub-

---

The author teaches in the Department of Economics, Northwestern University.

sidization of food (about 10 percent of GNP); and evidence that suggests post-harvest waste reduces gross agricultural production by 25 percent.[3] The causes of the weaknesses are linked to the limited authority collective and state farms have over input and output decisions because of the Communist Party's desire to maintain its control over the rural population and the distribution of agricultural output, and territorially separate, but nonetheless centralized and bureaucratic management of agriculture.

Even if collective and state farms were not forced to engage in bureaucratic bargaining, but rather in profit maximization, they would still face poor micro incentives due to inappropriate prices, profit leveling, an unstable regulatory environment, and an industrial sector uninterested in meeting the needs of agriculture. Thus, if decentralization of agricultural decision-making authority occurs without improved micro incentives, many agricultural problems will remain unsolved.

The status quo of Soviet agriculture is deplorable, yet is defended by an array of vested interests. Consumers oppose government efforts to raise agricultural retail prices, which would reduce food subsidies but also fuel inflationary pressure. The party is unwilling, for both ideological and pragmatic reasons, to let rural incomes outstrip urban incomes. Moreover, the party is concerned that more geographically uniform (and economically rational) regulation of agriculture would lead to much greater inequality in the distribution of rural income, which would then create ethnic unrest. Simply put, the authorities fear rebellion if a radical, market-oriented reform is implemented, yet the failure to implement such a reform, not only in agriculture but also in the rest of the economy, is slow death for the Soviet people.

Thus the questions that need to be answered are:

• How can decision-making authority be shifted to those "who till the land" without causing inflation, urban discontent, regional rural jealousies, and implacable party opposition?

• Once decision making has been decentralized, how can decentralized agricultural units receive the correct scarcity signals and the appropriate set of inputs from industry?

• Once the correct scarcity signals are in place, how can rural unemployment be avoided as unprofitable agricultural units are eliminated?

Later in this paper we will discuss the extent to which Hungary has been able to answer these questions correctly.

The Attractive Features of Hungarian Agriculture

Hungarian agriculture has had a solid reputation within the Soviet Union because of:
- Hungary's abundant self-sufficiency in agricultural goods;
- Hungary's decision to allow agricultural cooperatives and state farms to engage in nontraditional industrial, trade, and construction activities that have contributed to more efficient utilization of rural land and labor;
- an extensive large-scale socialist agricultural sector that has interacted effectively with Hungary's numerous small-scale producers;
- industrial production systems (or technically operating production systems) in agriculture that have created competitive conditions and have stimulated technological diffusion throughout Hungary;
- the opening up of marketing opportunities throughout Hungary that has encouraged producers to introduce new food products in response to increased competition;
- high yields for corn and wheat;
- reduction in food subsidies; and
- reduction in subsidies for industrial inputs into the agricultural sector.

Nonetheless, many Soviet agricultural specialists are reluctant to put much faith in Hungarian experience because Hungary is a small country in which: (a) land was never nationalized; (b) output prices for grains are crop-specific and not differentiated according to land quality; and (c) input and output prices are set on a national level, not on a regional level. Moreover, Hungarian agriculture can be criticized for its inefficient use of industrial inputs and stagnation during the 1980s. One sign of problems in Hungarian agriculture is that real income per collective farm worker declined by 10.4 percent between 1981 and 1988—even more rapidly than the 8.3 percent decline for nonagricultural wage earners (KSE 1988, 225).

Other more general signs that the Hungarian path of economic reform has been filled with many pitfalls include the following dimensions of Hungary's macro failure:
- slow growth of national income;
- large debt to the West;
- inefficient domestic utilization of energy and raw materials;
- a low level of competitiveness on world markets due to short-

sighted government policies;
  • a much weaker relative position in the world economy today than in 1970;
  • poverty among pensioners; and
  • inflation.

Perhaps most frightening for the Soviet Union is that the Hungarian road to reform has led to the abandonment of socialism and the disappearance of the Communist Party. In addition, a much less egalitarian distribution of income and wealth has become the norm.

The Evolution of Hungarian Agricultural Policy since 1965

During 1965–1967, Hungary's decentralizing reform efforts began in agriculture. Obligatory plan targets instituted by county and district authorities were abandoned in 1965 and farm units were allowed to determine their own production plans except with respect to grain production. Up until 1966, state purchasing prices for agricultural commodities were set so that cooperatives and state farms covered their expenses but were not able to finance their own expansion. In 1966, government purchasing prices of wheat and animal products were raised by about 9–10 percent. The largest price increases were for milk, beef, and pork—items also produced on household plots. In 1967, government supervision of cooperatives was substantially reduced. Cooperatives could now introduce levels of regularly timed wage payments, eliminate nonworking members, improve pension benefits, institute greater performance-related wage differentiation, and consolidate ownership over their own land.

This period also marks the beginning of the government's change in attitude toward the private plot. Restrictions on the sale of small machinery and tools, and on the granting of credit to private-plot farmers, came to an end. The government realized that private-plot production increased the standard of living of the rural population, contributed toward greater agricultural supplies for the urban population, industry and exports, and added to the state's tax base. Moreover, to the extent that private-plot farmers acquired land, credit, fodder, seed, tools, fertilizers, marketing facilities, and transportation from the collective, the interdependence between the private sector and the collective sector was strengthened.

This change in attitude reflected the government's realization that the rural population's enthusiastic participation in cooperative agriculture was a necessary ingredient for reaping the full benefits of economies of scale, while small-scale private-plot activity centered on commodities not characterized by economies of scale. The regulatory environment of agricultural cooperatives became similar to that of state farms because the ideological distinctions between the two organizational forms were considered of secondary importance with the realization that both are forms of socialist ownership. To put agricultural cooperatives on a more equal footing with state farms, 60 percent of the outstanding credits owed by the cooperative sector to the state was cancelled in 1967.

With the formal introduction of the New Economic Mechanism (NEM) in 1968, agricultural reform continued. Cooperatives were given greater decision-making authority: the right of the members to elect their officers in secret ballots; the ability (because of newly established development funds) and authority to purchase sophisticated machinery; the option to continue dealing with the recently increased number of state buying agencies, or directly signing contracts with state processing enterprises, or selling certain products on the open market (the introduction of the so-called multichannel sales system); and, for some cooperatives, the right to negotiate with and export directly to Western firms. Members of cooperatives now had the power to decide on inputs, outputs, and distribution.

State farms were also given greater decision-making latitude, and were encouraged to make decisions based on expected profitability. Both state farms and agricultural cooperatives were now interested in international agricultural markets. Before the introduction of the NEM, foreign sales of agricultural goods resulted in the domestic price being paid to the domestic producer. Beginning in 1968, agricultural enterprises received for their product the price paid by the international buyer, converted to forints by the newly introduced "uniform foreign-trade multipliers." In addition, some of the prices of agricultural products purchased by state agencies were allowed to respond to changes in demand and supply.

The amount of bureaucratic interaction that both state farms and agricultural cooperatives had to face was reduced by institutional changes. The Ministry of Agriculture and the Ministry of Food were merged into the Ministry of Agriculture and Food. The work week on state farms was officially reduced to 48 hours. However, financial incentives were introduced to encourage members of agricultural cooperatives to work longer hours. No longer was the wage bill of agricultural cooperatives regulated; members were now allowed to work as many hours as they wished. Furthermore, agricultural cooperatives were not required to pay profits tax; rather, they paid a differential income tax depending on per capita personal incomes. But, in addition, a tax on "incremental income" was devised to keep the personal incomes of cooperatives workers within planned limits. If the increase in the monthly average income per man-hour on a particular cooperative was above some norm, then a progressive tax was applied. This tax was used solely to subsidize the incomes of those working at cooperatives with unfavorable input endowments.

A differential land tax, progressive in terms of land quality, was introduced to reduce income differentials linked to differences in endowments of land. Also about one-third of all cooperatives received state subsidies to compensate them for the unfavorable conditions they faced.

Private-plot farmers also benefited from the decentralizing spirit of the NEM. Fodder, fertilizers, and pesticides were now sold commercially in quantities designed for the private plot. Larger quantities of small-scale machinery and tools were available. The legal restrictions on the number of animals permitted on private plots were abandoned and credit opportunities were extended to purchase livestock and to modernize stables.

Despite these reforms, agriculture and industry were being treated differently. Agricultural prices were consciously kept artificially low (relative to both production costs and world market prices) primarily to maintain domestic consumer-price stability and to avoid unacceptable income differentials between industrial and agricultural workers. This policy led to different taxation policies toward agricultural units because they earned smaller net incomes than industrial enterprises: agricultural units were not required to pay the wage tax, the charge on assets, and certain profit taxes.

With the initiation of a decentralized economic environment designed to stimulate agricultural productivity, the next step was to introduce up-to-date technology. Starting in 1970, technically operated production systems (TOPS) were developed by a number of large-scale farms, initially and most successfully for crop farming and later for horticulture and animal farming. Each TOPS headquarters is: (a) a self-financing franchiser that competitively sells detailed input-output programs and consulting services to large-scale farms that have complete freedom in deciding which, if any, TOPS to utilize for a particular product; (b) a channel for the transfer of international agribusiness techniques into Hungary; and (c) a substitute for the marketing services of Western agricultural suppliers and a complement to the information and research services of Hungary's Minister of Agriculture and Food Products.

The 1970s also witnessed the goals of small-scale farming shifting from self-sufficiency to market-oriented commodity production. The share of small-scale farming in agricultural gross output grew from 8.4 percent in 1970 to 9.6 percent in 1980, while small-scale agriculture's share of agriculture's total fixed capital stock dropped from 14.4 percent to 11.2 percent. Given that 70 percent of this output growth occurred on auxiliary farms, it is likely that an increase in the labor services of auxiliary farmers (whose primary jobs are not in agriculture) was a major reason for the expansion. Crucial to this increased labor effort were improved material incentives and permanent availability of inputs for small-scale farming. For example, by the early 1980s most cooperatives and state farms had established separate departments to provide capital services, materials, marketing, consulting, and transportation to small-scale producers.

Next, nonbasic agricultural activities such as food processing, construction, and trade activities were selected for rapid growth on large-scale farms in the early 1970s to: (a) provide jobs for underutilized rural labor during the late fall and winter and for those rural workers being replaced by mechanization; (b) give farms, especially those with poor-quality land, access to new profit sources, thus reducing their dependence on state subsidies; and (c) exploit the potential for profitable vertical integration in agriculture. Much of Hungary's success in nonbasic agriculture has been due to centrally determined incentives and to the ability of large-scale farms to organize nonbasic activities around either relatively inexpensive new technology or purchasable "used" machinery from industry.

In the 1980s, investment subsidies declined greatly, forcing farms to invest greater proportions of their own resources into any investment project. In addition, agricultural producers' prices lagged behind industrial producers' prices and the prices of imported agricultural inputs. Thus the profitability of traditional agricultural activities moved downward in the 1980s.

Firms reacted to this decline in profitability and to the incentives to engage in nonbasic agricultural activity by initiating mergers designed to promote vertical integration. Simultaneously, the government broke up most of the food monopolies into potentially competitive independent enterprises.

Unfortunately, agricultural subsidies to promote hard-currency exports and to support farms with low-quality land continued to play a role in Hungarian agriculture throughout the 1980s as Hungary focused on its short-term needs, even though the long-term rationale for such subsidization was weak.

The Limited Applicability of Hungarian Experience

Returning to the questions posed above, Hungary succeeded in decentralizing agricultural decision making without igniting a revolution due to five factors. First, financial incentives replaced mandatory plan targets *and* these financial incentives were sufficiently attractive to enable the rural standard of living to improve steadily. For instance, not only did the individual incomes of rural individuals increase, but local taxation and centrally designed profit regulation led to a general upgrading of rural roads, schools, hospitals, and so forth. The readily apparent increase in the wealth of rural communities mitigated opposition by local authorities. However, urban discontent surfaced in the early 1970s and agricultural decentralization came to a standstill for a while. Second, land taxes and crop-specific price supplements for farms with poor-quality land were used to curb regional rural jealousies. Over time, land taxes became more important and price supplements less important. Third, agricultural subsidies gradually declined amid centrally orchestrated public debate about the need for and rationale behind the cutback in subsidies. Subsidies for agricultural inputs and for investment funding disappeared more quickly than subsidies designed to promote more egalitarian rural incomes and to protect consumers from higher food prices. Nonetheless, loud complaints were voiced by all parties during the reduction of subsidies. Fourth, food prices were decontrolled step-by-step. For a long period of time, consumer prices rose in concert with compensating wage increases. Later, market prices were allowed to prevail. Fifth, government authorities actively reduced the agricultural bureaucracy, allowed for organizational innovation, and eventually sought to promote competition by breaking up monopolies in the food industry.

Next, Hungary avoided unemployment in rural areas by promoting nonbasic agricultural activity and encouraging the mutually beneficial interaction of large-scale and small-scale agriculture. Unfortunately, Hungary did not introduce scarcity signals based on world market prices into the agricultural sector because of the perceived need to reach short-term export targets and not long-term development goals. This short-sightedness not only influenced agriculture, but the rest of the economy as well.

Thus the Soviet Union should not be as inward-looking as Hungary has been in terms of influencing scarcity prices. Soviet agriculture has taken one step toward an outward-looking policy by offering to pay Soviet collective and state farms in convertible currency for deliveries above each farm's "norm" delivery of durum and strong wheat, peas, lupine, and oilseed.[5]

In the Soviet Union, there have also been discussions pointing toward transforming unprofitable collective and state farms into parcels that could be leased via a contract system from the government. Such a policy would assist the Soviet Union in avoiding the negative incentive effects of profit-leveling which have contributed toward the inefficiency of Hungarian agriculture. However, since Soviet leasing policies have thus far implied loss of income and power for the management of collective and state farms, leasing has not yet been widely successful.

Positive Lessons

The first lesson that Hungary offers is that agriculture must undergo a comprehensive reform, rather than limited incentives designed to increase profit awareness. A comprehensive reform should include:

• uniform output and input prices throughout the Soviet Union, plus the introduction of land taxes. Unresolved problems of differential land quality and weather conditions can be temporarily mitigated with lump-sum subsidies that would decrease over time and with incentives to engage in nonbasic agricultural activities. Over time, regional specialization should increase and unproductive land should not be utilized as farm land. The output and input prices should reflect international opportunity costs, not domestic production costs.

• a steady decrease in food subsidies with a simultaneous effort to increase the wage level of the population to compensate for the higher retail food prices.

• the promotion of large-scale and small-scale agriculture via the introduction of incentive schemes that would allow individual farmers, managers of collective and state farms, and local party and government officials to share in untapped rural profits. Necessary conditions for cooperation between small-scale producers and large-scale farms include government decisions to let industrious peasants become wealthy and to funnel a significant share of the profits of collective and state farms to public goods projects in neighboring rural communities.

• the dramatic shrinkage of the bureaucracy that deals with agriculture. However, there should be sufficient funds available to import agricultural goods in case the early transition difficulties produce even worse shortages than currently exist. Unless the bureaucracy is disbanded, it will interfere in the decisions of agricultural units.[6]

• allowing a wide diversity of organizational forms to develop voluntarily.

The second lesson that Hungarian experience highlights is that a successful agrarian policy can bolster the population's faith in the Communist Party. Even though the Hungarian Socialist Workers' Party has been recently disbanded, the success Hungary enjoyed in agriculture during the 1960s and 1970s strengthened the Hungarian population's belief in the viability of their own economic system. If the Communist Party of the Soviet Union is to survive in a democratic environment, it must implement an agrarian policy that leads to the revitalization of rural regions throughout the Soviet Union. Hungary accomplished this. Such revitalization in the Soviet Union would greatly lessen ethnic unrest and thus increase the viability of perestroika.

Notes

1. "In the Politburo of the CPSU Central Committee," *Current Digest of the Soviet Press* (CDSP), XLI, no. 9: 20–21.

2. "How Much Is a Ruble Worth?" CDSP, XLI, no. 36:26–27 from *Izvestiia* September 9, 1989: 1; "From One Payday to the Next," CDSP, XLI, no. 35: 23–24 from *Izvestia*, September 21, 1989: 1.

3. *CPE*, I, no. 6 (November/December, 1988): 4.

4. Much of this material comes from Marrese (1983, 1986) and Fekete (1989).

5. The norm for wheat is the 1981–85 farm-specific average, for peas and

lupine the 1986–88 farm-specific average, and for oilseeds the 1986–88 farm-specific average provided that total sales of all of a farm's oilseeds exceed the 1986–88 average. "Foreign Currency for Farmers," CDSP, XLI, no. 33:32 from *Pravda*, August 19, 1989: 2; "Soviet Government to Pay Farmers in Foreign Exchange for Part of their Output," *RSEEA*, vol. 11, issue 3, September 1989: 2.

6. Thus far, Soviet agricultural bureaucracy has not shrunk; it has just changed hats. For example, the USSR State Agro-Industrial Committee was abolished in spring 1989, then its functions were assigned to the State Planning Committee, the State Supply Committee, the State Committee on Labor and Wages, and the Ministry of Foreign Economic Relations. See "The USSR State Agro-Industrial Committee Departs the Scene," CDSP, XLI, no. 15:25 from *Izvestiia*, April 11, 1989: 1.

References

Brada, Josef C., and Karl-Eugen Wädekin, eds. (1988). *Socialist Agriculture in Transition: Organizational Response to Failing Performance*. Boulder and London: Westview Press.

CDSP (weekly), *Current Digest of the Soviet Press*.

CPE (bimonthly), *CPE Agricultural Report*. Washington, DC: US Department of Agriculture, Centrally Planned Economies Branch, Agriculture and Trade Analysis Division.

Fekete, Ferene (1989). "Progress and Problems in Hungarian Agriculture." In *Hungary: The Second Decade of Economic Reform*, ed. Roger A. Clarke, pp. 59–74. Essex, UK: Longman.

KSE (annual volumes), *Külkereskedelmi Statisztikai Évkönyv* [Hungarian Foreign-Trade Statistical Yearbook]. Budapest: Központi Statisztikai Hivatal.

Marrese, Michael (1983). "Agricultural Policy and Performance in Hungary." *Journal of Comparative Economics* 7, 3: 329–45.

——— (1986). "Hungarian Agriculture: Moving in the Right Direction." In *East European Economics: Slow Growth in the 1980s*, Joint Economic Committee of the US Congress. Washington, DC: US Government Printing Office, Vol. 3, pp. 322–340 (March).

Narkhoz (annual volumes) *Narodnoe khoziaistvo SSSR v 19— g.: Statisticheskii ezhegodnik* [National Economy of the USSR in 19—: Statistical Yearbook]. Moscow: Finansy i statistika.

RSEEA (quarterly) *Newsletter for Research on Soviet and East European Agriculture*. Portland, Maine: University of Southern Maine.

Wädekin, Karl-Eugen (1989). "Prospects for Soviet Agriculture: Some Less Noticed Aspects." Paper presented at the 1989 NATO Colloquium, "Soviet Economic Reforms: Implementation Under Way," Brussels, March 15–17.

Index

Abolition of serfdom (1861), 3, 9
Accounting. *See* Khozraschet
Adazhi (agrofirm), 25–26, 44*n. 26*
Administrative intervention, 56
Administrirovanie, 34
Adylov, 84
Aganbegyan, Abel, 78
Agro-association, 38, 40, 43
  management of, 26–27
  RAPO and, 26
Agrofirm, 21, 24, 40, 43
  management of, 25–26
Agro-Industrial Bank
  (Agroprombank), 59
Agrokombinat, 21, 38, 40, 43
  management of, 24–25
Agropromstroi, 38, 40
Akkord, 87–88
All Union Scientific Research Institute
  for Agricultural Economics, 69
Altai krai, 33
Anan'ev, Anatolii, 102
Andreeva, Nina, 100
  letter by, 96
Andropov, Yuri, 90
Animal products, 119
Apparat/apparatchiki, 19, 83
Arenda, law on the, 87
Arendator, 87, 89, 103*n. 8*
Arendnyi podriad. *See* Lease
  contracts
Arkhangelsk oblast, 39–40
Article 87, 11
Associations of cooperatives, 27
Azerbaijan, 33, 40

Bailouts, 48
Baltic republics, 55, 61
Banking system, agricultural financing
  and, 24
Bankruptcy, 29, 48, 59

Bashmachnikov, Vladimir, 97
Basic Law of the USSR and Union
  Republics on Leasing, 72
Beef, 119. *See also* Meat products
Belgorod oblast, 90, 100
Belorussia, 34
Beznariadnaia system, 88
Bonuses, 34, 59, 64, 76–77
  profits and, 52–53
Brezhnev, Leonid, 79, 90
Brezhnev period, 48, 51, 53, 60, 91, 98
Brigades and brigade contracts, 85, 98
  akkord system and, 88
  in Belgorod, 100
  contract leasing and, 89–90
  decline of, in late 1980s, 76–77
  family contract and, 92–93
  Gorbachev and campaign for, 91
Budget, agricultural, 50–51
Bukharin, Nikolai, 7
Bunich, Pavel, 86
Bureaucracy, 112, 117, 125
  agricultural policy and, 31, 36–41
  agricultural reforms and, 8–9, 13
  Gosagroprom and, 37
  Hungarian agriculture and, 120–121,
    123–124

Campaigns for lease contracts, 90–98,
  101–102
Campaigns, administrative, 81–85
Cattle prices, 112
Central authority, reforms and, 10–11
Cheliabinsk oblast, 40
Chernenko, Konstantin, 91
Chernobyl disaster, 68
China, 48, 55, 60, 61, 112–113
Chita oblast, 40
Cochrane, Glynn, 42
Coefficient of labor participation
  (KTU), 76–77

Coherence, policy, 31–32
Collective contracts, 33, 76–78
Collective farms. *See* Kolkhozy
Collective tradition in Russia,
    agricultural reforms and, 7
Collectivization, 4, 16, 28, 81
Commodity pricing zones, 59
Common Agricultural Program, 110
Communes, peasant, 3, 7, 9, 11–12
Communication, agricultural policy
    and, 31–32
Communist Party of the Soviet Union,
    117, 125
Communist Party Central Committee,
    23, 90, 92
Communist Party Central Committee
    Plenum (July 1988), 24, 76
Communist Party Central Committee
    Plenum (September 1988), 96
Communist Party Central Committee
    Plenum (March 1989), 24, 43*n. 2,*
    45*n. 40,* 67–68, 71, 78
Communist Party Conference (1988), 35
Communist Party Congress,
    Twenty-seventh (1986), 81, 90–91
Competition, 42
Congress of Kolkhozniks (March
    1988), 95
Congress of People's Deputies, 102
Conservatism, agricultural reforms
    and, 20
Construction, Hungarian agriculture
    and, 122
Contracts
  collective, 33, 76–78
  fixed-rent, 65–66
  free, 66
  individual, 93
  lease. *See* Lease contracts
  share, 65–66
  wage, 64–65, 78–79
Convertible ruble, 56
Cooperative organizations in tsarist
    Russia, 7
Cooperatives, agricultural, 56
  associations of, 27
  in Hungary, 118–120, 122
  law on, 78
Corn, 111, 118

Cost accounting. *See* Khozraschet
Costs of reforms, 10
Cotton, 112
Council of Ministers, 56–57
Council of People's Deputies (rural),
    69, 73, 74
Credits, agricultural, 49, 51, 64. *See
    also* Financing, agricultural
  policy, 59
Cuba, 109

Dagestan, 24
Dairy products, 108–109, 113
  eggs, 112
  milk, 119
Debt, 53, 63
  collective farms and, 48–50
  Gorbachev and, 67–68
  write-off of, 50, 79*n. 2*
Decentralization, 117
  Hungarian agriculture and, 119,
    123
Disbandment of farms, 29
Disposition
  agricultural policy and, 31, 34–36
  education and, 35–36
Distribution of income, 116
Distribution of land, 74–75
Duma, 11

Education, 41
  agricultural, 32–33
  disposition and, 35–36
Eggs, 112. *See also* Dairy products
Ekabpils (Latvia), 26
Ekonomicheskaia gazeta, 25
Elites, Soviet, agricultural reforms
    and, 19, 100
Emel'ianov, A. M., 73–74
Estonia, 24, 42
European Community (EC), 110–111,
    114
Exchange rate for tourists, 114
Exports, agricultural, 107. *See also*
    Trade, agricultural
  Hungarian experience and, 123

Family-based leasing, 81–82, 85. *See
    also* Lease contracts

brigade contract and, 92–93
political issues and, 98–101
Family plots. *See* Household plots
Far East, Soviet, 33
Farm independence, 36–37
Farms, private, 55
Fertilizers, 58, 121
Filatov, A. P., 104*n. 14*
Financial-accounting center, 24
Financing, agricultural, 47–48, 60–61, 67–68
crisis in, 48–50
financially unhealthy farms and, 28–29
future reforms and, 57–59
inefficient investment allocation and, 50–53
internal banking system and, 24
perestroika and, 53–57
RAPO and, 37
self-financing and, 55–56, 58
Five-Year-Plan (1990), 58
Fixed-rent contracts, 65–66
Fodder, 121
Food prices, retail, 113, 117
in Hungary, 123
Food processing, Hungarian agriculture and, 122
Food production
agricultural reforms and, 20
perestroika and, 30
RAPO and, 22
Food Program (1982), 67
Food Program (1983), 50
Fragmentation, problem of, in agricultural management, 39–40
Free contracts, 66

GATT, 114
Gorbachev, Mikhail, 26, 28, 43*n. 2,* 45*n. 40,* 92, 104*n. 10*
agricultural reforms and, 81–82, 90–91, 93–97
agrokombinats and, 25
collective contracts and, 76, 78
collective farms and, 99–101
compared with Stolypin, 5–18
farm debts and, 67–68
perestroika and, 19

Gosagroprom, 21, 22, 30, 78, 90, 97
bureaucracy and, 37
of Latvia, 104*n. 10*
lease contracts and, 86, 96
vysshaia shkola of, 33–34
Gradualist reforms, 15–16
Grain, 108–112
corn, 111, 118
rice, 108
wheat, 108, 110, 111, 118, 119, 124, 125*n. 5*
Guizot, 7

Hog prices, 112
Household plots, 12
in Hungarian agriculture, 119–121
lease contracts and, 68–69
Hungarian agriculture, 71, 116
attractive features of, 118–119
construction and, 122
food processing and, 122
household plots and, 119–121
limited applicability of experience of, 123–124
policy since 1965, 119–123
positive lessons of, 124–125
taxation and, 121, 123
Hungarian Socialist Workers' Party, 125

Imports, agricultural, 107–108. *See also* Trade, agricultural
USSR import bill and, 109–111
Incentives, 34–35, 52, 58, 63, 64–65, 111, 117, 125
agricultural reforms and, 7
Hungarian agriculture and, 121–123
Income distribution, 116
Independence of farms, 36–37
Individual contracts, 93
Individualism
absence of tradition of, in Russian agriculture, 12–13
agricultural reforms' contribution to, 7
Individual enterprise, law on, 92
Individual proprietorship, 64, 73. *See also* Ownership, land
Inefficiency, lease contracting and, 54
Inflation, 50, 56, 59, 71, 116, 117

Infrastructure
  agricultural, 111
  transportation, 31–32
Innovation campaigns, 82–83
Intensive Labor Collectives (KITy), 93
Interest payments, 49
Interkolkhoz construction
    organizations, 38
Internal banking system, 24
Intrafarm leases, 87, 99
Investments, agricultural, 58
  inefficiency in allocation of, 50–53
  reforms and, 83–84
Israel, Arturo, 42
Izvestiia, 97

Joint-stock companies, farms managed
    as, 29–30

Kalnyn'sh, 44*n. 26*
Karaganda, 100–101
Khozraschet (cost-accounting), 33–34, 98
Khrushchev, Nikita, 78, 87
Khutor, 7, 12, 16
Kirgizia, 33
Kolkhoz Model Charter, 103*n. 2*
Kolkhozy (collective farms), 14, 28,
    84, 85, 93, 103*n. 2,* 103*n. 3,* 112,
    125
  agricultural reform and, 7–9, 15, 54,
    94–97
  contract leasing and, 55, 65–66, 75,
    87–88
  debt and, 48–50
  family-based leases and, 81–82
  Gorbachev and, 99–101
  Ligachev and, 99–100
  Tikhonov's proposals and, 57
  wages on, 67
Kommunist, 35, 96
Kostroma oblast, 100
Krasnodar, 24
Krasnodar krai, 24–25, 100
Kuban' (agrokombinat), 24–25

Land
  distribution of, 74–75
  leasing of. *See* Lease contracts
  legislation on, 65, 72–73, 102

ownership of, 3–4, 72–73
  payments on, 59
  quality of, 71
  taxation on, 61
Latvia, 23, 24, 25–26, 42
Latvian Gosagroprom, 104*n. 10*
Law on Cooperatives, 78
Law on Individual Enterprise, 92
Law on land, 65, 72, 102
Law on land tenure, 56–57
Law on leasing, 74–75, 98
Law on ownership, 73
Law on the Arenda, 87
Lease contracts, 61, 63, 65–68,
    86–90, 103*n. 5,* 103*n. 7,* 104*n.
    14,* 124
  campaigns for, 90–98, 101–102
  collective contracts and, 76–78
  collective farms and, 55, 65–66, 75
  inefficient farms and, 54
  legal foundation for, 72–76, 98
  legislation and, 56–57
  political issues and, 98–101
  terms of, 68–72
Lease sub-contract, 87
Lease teams, 54–55
Leases
  and farm management, 28–30
  targeted, 65–66
Leasing, family-based. *See*
    Family-based leasing
Legislation, 56–57, 63, 86–87. *See*
    also specific laws, above
  agricultural reforms and, 11
  intra-organizational regulations and
    procedures and, 36–38
  leasing and proprietorship and, 72–76
Lenin, Vladimir, 90
Lenin Agricultural Academy (Siberian
    branch), 34
Lenin All-Union Academy of
    Agricultural Sciences. *See*
    VASKhNIL
Ligachev, Yegor, 29, 93, 97, 104*n. 14*
  collective farms and, 99–100
Lin, Justin Yifu, 64
Lithuania, 75–76
Livestock, production of, 110. *See*
    also Meat products

Loans, short-term, 49
Lupine, 124
Lvov, 30

Machinery, small-scale agricultural, in Hungary, 121
Management, agricultural. *See also* Policy, agricultural; Reforms, agricultural
  agro-association and, 26–27
  agrofirm, 25–26
  agrokombinat and, 24–25
  fragmentation in, 39–40
  Gorbachev and, 94
  in Hungary, 120–121
  leases and, 28–30
  other raion-level management organizations and, 27–28
  RAPO and, 21–24
  reforms and, 20–21, 30–31
Managers, farm, 75
  lease contracts and, 66–69
Markets, 56, 61
  agricultural reforms and, 117
  Hungarian agriculture and, 118, 122
Meat and Dairy Ministry, 40
Meat products, 108, 109, 113
  beef, 119
  pork, 119
Milk, 119. *See also* Dairy products
Minimum wage, 52
Ministries, RAPO and, 21–23
Ministry of Foreign Economic Relations, 126*n. 6*
Minselstroi, 38
Mogilev oblast, 26
Moscow, 25
Moscow oblast, 25, 58
Murakhovskii, 97, 104*n. 11*

Nagornyi Dagestan (kombinat), 24
New Economic Mechanism (NEM), Hungarian agriculture and, 120–121
New Economic Policy (NEP), 4, 16, 90
Nikonov, Aleksandr A., 56, 95
Nikonov, Viktor, 23–24, 27, 44*n. 37,* 93, 96, 99

Nomenklatura, 35
Non-Black Soil Zone, 51, 54, 66, 92
Novomoskovskii raion, 26
Novomoskovskoe agro-association, 26–27
Novosibirsk, 34
Novosibirsk oblast, 104*n. 14*
NPO, 38

Oblast, 43*n. 5*
Oilseeds, 109, 110, 112, 124, 126*n. 5*
Omsk, 29
Orel oblast, 100
Orenburg oblast, 85
Organization, agricultural. *See* Management, agricultural; Policy, agricultural; Reforms, agricultural
Organizational resources, 32–34
Orlovskaia oblast, 69, 77
Ownership, land
  individual proprietorship, 64, 73
  legislation and, 72–73
  in tsarist Russia, 3–4

Partiinaia zhizn', 35
Party district committee. *See* Raikom
Peas, 124, 125*n. 5*
Peasant communes, 3, 7, 9, 11–12
Peasants, cultivation of land by, in tsarist period, 3–4
Perestroika, 19, 30, 36, 41, 82, 116, 125
  agricultural financing and, 53–57
  agricultural reforms and, 20
  campaigns for lease contracts and, 101–102
  food production and, 30
  Gorbachev and, 19
Pesticides, 121
Peter the Great, 10
Plemob"edineniia, 38
Poland, 55, 56
Policy, agricultural. *See also* Management, agricultural; Reforms, agricultural
  bureaucracy and, 31, 36–41
  coherence of, 31–32
  communication and, 31–32
  disposition and, 31, 34–36

organizational resources and, 32–34
Politburo, 5
  agrokombinats and, 25
Political stability, agricultural reforms
    and, 5–6
Pork, 119. *See also* Meat products
Pravda, 33, 35, 82, 92
Price policy, 58
Price reform, 60, 113
Prices and pricing, 29, 55, 56, 88, 89,
    111, 124
  for cattle, 112
  contract, 69
  fixed rent contracts and, 65–66
  in Hungary, 121–123
  policies, 59
  procurement, 59, 61
  retail, 113, 117
  trade liberalization and, 107–109
Private farms, 55
Production associations (POs), 38
Production systems, technically
    operated (TOPS), 121–122
Profits, 29, 58, 117
  bonuses and, 52–53
  farm, 50
  Hungarian agriculture and, 122–123
  lease contracts and, 65, 69–71
  subsidies and, 50, 56
  targeted lease contracts and, 66
Proprietorship, individual, 64, 73
Ptitsepromy, 38

Radical reforms, 15
Radio Moscow, 40
Raig, Ivar, 55
Raikom (Party district committee), 35,
    41, 82–83
  RAPO and, 22–23
Raion, 27–28, 43*n. 4*
Ramenskii agrokombinat, 25
RAPO, 20–24, 29, 30, 33, 38–42
  agro-association and, 26
  agrokombinat and, 24–25
  financing and, 37
  food production and, 22
Rassvet (agrofirm), 26
Rationing, 111
Reforms, agricultural, 19–20. *See*

also Management, agricultural;
    Policy, agricultural
  central authority and, 10–11
  collective tradition in Russia and, 7
  conservatism and, 20
  costs of, 10
  differences of Stolypin, compared
      with Gorbachev, 14
  financing and, 57–59
  food production and, 20
  gradualism and, 15–16
  Hungarian experience and, 123–125
  implementation of, under Stolypin
      compared with Gorbachev, 5–8
  intra-organizational regulations and,
      36–38
  investments and, 83–84
  kolkhozy and, 7–9, 15, 54, 94–97
  management and, 20–21, 30–31
  obstacles to, 116–117
  overview, 3–5
  perestroika and, 20
  political stability and, 5–6
  problems facing Stolypin, compared
      with Gorbachev, 8–14
  social equity and, 12
  Stolypin's prospects for success,
      compared with Gorbachev, 14–18
Regulations, intra-organizational
  agricultural reforms and, 36–38
Rental fees, 69, 72
Resources
  agricultural policy and, 31
  allocation of, 51
Retail prices, 113, 117
Revolution of 1905, 4, 6
Rice, 108
Rostov, 24
Rostov oblast, 40
Ruble, 111
  as convertible currency, 56
  tourist exchange rate for, 114
Russian Republic, 55–56, 57, 58, 66
Russian Republic agro-industrial bank,
    29
Ryzhkov, Nikolai, 56, 78, 99

Sel'skaia zhizn' (newspaper), 23, 35
Self-financing, 55–56, 58

Serfdom, abolition of (1861), 3, 9
Share contracts, 65–66
Sheep farms, 33
Shmelev, Gelii, 85
Shortages, 54, 60, 116–117
Siberia, 13, 33, 54, 85
Siberian rivers diversion project, 91–92, 98
Sobchak, A. A., 73–74
Sochi, 24–25
Social equity, agricultural reforms and, 12
Soviet Far East, 33
Soviets, 57
Sovkhozy (state farms), 28, 84, 85, 87–88, 103*n. 3,* 112, 125
  debt and, 48–50
  family-based leases and, 81–82
  Gorbachev and, 99–101
  lease contracting and, 55, 65–66, 75
  reorganization of, 29–30, 54, 93–96
Spare parts, 31
Stalin, Joseph, 4, 81
Stalinism, 43*n. 2*
State Agro-Industrial Committee, USSR, 126*n. 6*
State Committee on Labor and Wages, 126*n. 6*
State farms. *See also* Sovkhozy
  in Hungarian agriculture, 118, 120, 122
State Planning Committee, 126*n. 6*
State Supply Committee, 126*n. 6*
Stavropol, 34
Stavropol krai, 24, 34, 100
Stolypin, Petr
  differences compared with Gorbachev, 14
  implementation of agricultural reforms compared to Gorbachev, 5–8
  problems faced by, compared with Gorbachev, 8–14
  prospects for success, compared with Gorbachev, 14–18
Stroev, Ygor, 96
Sub-contract, lease, 87
Subsidies, agricultural, 48, 55–56, 58–59, 61, 67, 116–118, 125
  Hungarian agriculture and, 123

profits and, 50, 56
Sugar, 108, 109
Supreme Soviet, USSR, 56
Sverdlovsk oblast, 27

Targeted leases, 65–66
Taxation, 124
  Hungarian agriculture and, 121, 123
  land tax, 61
Team principle, 64
Teams, lease, 54–55
Technically operated production systems (TOPS), 121–122
Technology, Hungarian agriculture and, 118, 122
Tenure, land. *See* Lease contracts
Three-field strip system, 3
Tikhonov, Vladimir A., 56–57, 97, 104*n. 11*
Timeshevskii raion, 24
Tourist exchange rate, 114
Trade, agricultural, 107, 114–115
  in Hungary, 122
  liberalization of, 111–114
  price effects of liberalization of, 107–109
  USSR import bill and, 109–111
Tradition, agricultural reforms and break with, 6–7
Training, agricultural, 32–33. *See also* Education
Transportation infrastructure, 31–32
Trusts, 38
Tselinograd oblast, 69
Tula oblast, 26

Ukraine, 32–33, 58, 93
Unemployment, 101
  Hungarian agriculture and, 124
  rural, 117
"Union of cooperatives" (Sverdlovsk oblast), 27
Union of Peasant Farmers and Agricultural Cooperatives of Russia, 103
United Nobility, 8
United States, 50, 114
  grain exports to USSR and, 110–111
Uzun, V. Ia., 85

VASKhNIL, 56, 104*n. 11*
Vegetable oils, 109
Vladimir oblast, 30
Vodka sales, 50
Volga region, 92
Volgograd, 24
Voronezh Oblast, 53
Vysshaia shkola (of Gosagroprom),
33–34

Wage contracts, 64–65, 78–79

Wages, 48, 55, 60, 79*n. 1*, 88, 103*n. 3*,
113, 125
collective contracts and, 77
on kolkhozy, 67
minimum wage, 52
Waste, 117
Wheat, 108, 110, 111, 118, 119, 124, 125*n. 5*
Witte, Count, 10
Work point system, 64

Zaslavskaia, Tat′iana, 93

About the Editor

WILLIAM MOSKOFF, D. K. Pearsons Professor of Economics at Lake Forest College, is editor of the journal *Comparative Economic Studies.* Author of *Labor and Leisure in the Soviet Union: Public and Private Decision-making in a Planned Economy* and *The Bread of Affliction: The Food Supply in the USSR during World War II,* Moskoff is also the coeditor (with Susan J. Linz) of *Reorganization and Reform in the Soviet Economy* and (with Anthony Jones) of *Perestroika and the Economy: New Thinking in Soviet Economics.* He is currently at work on a study of the development of cooperatives in the USSR.